The Survivalist

You Can Do It the Easy Way or the Hard Way

T0105673

THE SERENITY PRAYER

GOD, GRANT ME THE SERENITY TO ACCEPT THE THINGS I CANNOT CHANGE; THE COURAGE TO CHANGE THE THINGS I CAN; AND THE WISDOM TO KNOW THE DIFFERENCE

The Survivalist

You Can Do It the Easy Way or the Hard Way

◆◆◆◆

Larry Hager

iUniverse, Inc.

Bloomington

The Survivalist
You Can Do It the Easy Way or the Hard Way

iUniverse books may be ordered through booksellers or by contacting:

iUniverse
1663 Liberty Drive
Bloomington, IN 47403
www.iuniverse.com
1-800-Authors (1-800-288-4677)

ISBN: 978-1-4620-2009-6 (sc)
ISBN: 978-1-4620-2010-2 (e)

Printed in the United States of America

iUniverse rev. date: 05/20/2011

Contents

◇◇◇◇

INTRODUCTION

❖❖❖❖

This book is basically the story of my life to date. It starts out as the story of my family's life before I was born when they immigrated from Kansas and the dust bowl of the 30s to Idaho and then on to Oregon in 1939 after the supposed end of the Great Depression. Twelve years later when I was eight we moved to a small logging community in southern Oregon and a whole new life style for a little farm boy. There were a lot of interesting moments between the ages of 17 to 21 and most of them I would have been far better off avoiding, however I didn't, instead I seemed to embrace them and those early years just about wrecked my life.

My friends used to say that someday I would wind up in the penitentiary but I didn't believe them: when it happened, I don't think I really understood the seriousness of it for awhile; when I finally did understand I started doing some things with my life that would not only get me out but allow me to stay out.

After I was out about 3 years I found that what I really needed was a family; after I got that I knew I was going to be alright. There was; however, still decisions to be made and this time I had to get it right because now my family was depending on me.

Chapter One: My Father Was A Cowboy

❖❖❖❖

I was born In a Catholic Hospital in La Grande Oregon in 1942. My father was working as a cowboy on the John Davis Ranch just out of John Day Oregon. The Great Depression was supposed to be over but it was still having an effect. That is; people were poor, wages were low, the war effort was a huge help to the economy and at least there were some jobs to be had. Maybe not what you would normally have chosen but during and in the aftermath of the depression, folks weren't too particular. If you had a roof over your head and food to eat things weren't too bad and working on a cattle ranch gave dad a little cabin where he could raise and feed his little family and a new baby could be born.

In September 1939, after the end of what they called the "Great Depression" dad had brought his family west looking for work and after a few jobs such as working driving a potato truck, (my mother worked in the potato packing house cutting seed spuds) he had eventually landed a better paying job working for a large construction company driving a "Ute" dump truck building a road in the Blue mountains in Eastern

Oregon. They lived in a homemade 8 ft trailer; pulled by a Model A Ford coupe, on the banks of the Minam River. The construction crew and their families were living in tents and any shelters that they could devise there. One of my dad's brothers, his wife, and their daughter, who was probably about three, was there also, living in a tent. The women washed clothes in the river on the rocks.

My Grandparents moved from Kansas to Fruitland Idaho and bought a twenty acre farm before dad, mom, and my brother came west. Dad was never one to jump from the frying pan into the fire. I have read in the letters that they wrote to Grandma that they were thinking of making the move but they wanted to be fairly certain that things would be better once they did as they surely wouldn't have an opportunity for a do over.

My grandmother saved all of these letters and when my grandmother died somehow my mother came into possession of them. After my father had passed away and my mother had to be put in a nursing home I found them in a box in the attic in the old house. It is like reading a diary of a disaster. It makes me proud to have had these people for my parents when I read of the courage they needed to just survive another day and it is heart breaking to see the hard ships they had to endure with no way out. They actually were down to foraging for food such as wild greens in the ditches along the roads, wild mushrooms, and several different kinds of wild berries. This was still going on when I was a small boy, but by that time we had a large garden, but wild things were still on the table too. They were quite good really. I didn't feel in the least deprived. People who think that this era that we are living in is like the Great Depression are clueless. They should read some of

John Steinbeck's novels such as *The Grapes of Wrath*, or better yet, talk to some of the people who lived it. They might learn something. The thing that has the potential for making this worse though is that those people were tougher than most folks are today. They were able to survive with almost nothing and they thought that taking care of themselves and their family was their jobs not the governments or some social organization. I know that those years had a devastating effect on both of my parents. They never really recovered. Dad's biggest fear was that his family would starve, no matter how much money he had saved. Years later that was still all he could talk about.

My father was a fanatic about saving money and would go on and on about the virtues of compound interest. He had a limited education, 8th grade I believe, but he was intelligent and always made out his own income tax and did it right. Neither dad nor mother drank. That was a good thing, and he tried to be a good father but he thought that all that meant was making enough money to keep his family from going hungry. We had clothes to wear and food to eat and a roof over our heads but not a lot of unnecessary things. Once, years later, I brought a girlfriend to their house that was on welfare and had five children; and after they had left her teenage son said; "Mamma, we are supposed to be poor, why do we have nicer things than they do?" She told me this later and I had to admit he was right. We didn't get anything new as long as it was useable or it could be fixed or patched.

The first place that I remember living was in Union Oregon. That would have been about 1946. Union was a ranching town on the Old Oregon Trail. They still had cattle drives right past our house. Dad; however had found a job that paid more than being a cowboy, and was working at a saw mill in town riding the carriage and "dogging" and "ratchet setting". Those are terms used to describe how they sawed logs in those days. Men rode the carriage that carried the log back and forth past a saw that cut the log into boards. They moved the log out to cut the next board (*ratchet setting)* and hammered a cleat or dog into the log to hold it steady while it was being cut. (*dogging.)* This was a very dangerous job that is done now remotely by the sawyer with a computerized hydraulic cylinder system called *Temposonics*. The following spring dad went to work in the woods. He liked that a lot better. He could make more money. He fell and bucked big Ponderosa pine with a cross cut saw. He actually got paid according to how much work he did rather than being paid by the hour.

We lived on an old place on the edge of town where we had an orchard, a couple of milk cows and a calf or two; we also had chickens, turkeys, pigs, dogs and cats, and a big garden. We had no running water or indoor plumbing; and as did almost everyone in rural America in the 40s we also had an outhouse and a chamber pot under the bed that we would empty every morning. We had a wood cook stove and a bucket with a tin dipper hung on the side of it sitting on the counter top. We took our baths in the kitchen in a round galvanized washtub sitting on the floor next to the wood cook stove. The water came from a pitcher pump out in the yard and it was carried into the house in a bucket and heated on the cook stove. There were cook stoves out then that had a reservoir for heating water but we didn't have one. The way I remember it is that Momma took her bath then she gave me a bath, then my brother took his, then Dad. When the water cooled off too much there was a bucket of hot water sitting on the stove.

I suppose you could say that we were poor, but if we were then so were most working people. Our lifestyle was perfectly normal in rural America in the 30s and 40s.

I don't think anyone had ever heard of insulation in those days and it got way below zero there in the winter time. Nowadays people make quilts for a hobby but back then they were necessary. My brother and I wore long underwear and slept together to keep warm. We also had quilts and blankets piled on us so heavy that we could barely turn over. We would wake up in the morning with heavy frost on the inside of the windows. We had a pot bellied coal stove but it didn't put out much heat in that drafty old two story farm house and we couldn't afford to burn it all night anyway.

When I got up in the morning I would run for the kitchen. Momma would have a fire going in the wood cook stove and be baking bread and cinnamon rolls in the oven. Wow. The smells, the memories; I loved it. What a fun place to be a little boy.

I learned to ride a bike, my brother taught me; That is he put me on it and pushed me. I couldn't reach the pedals and when I fell over he would pick me up and put me back on and give me another push; eventually I learned the fine art of balance; however when I wanted to stop I still had to fall over unless I was next to a curb or a step so that I could touch. I don't think training wheels had been invented yet, and certainly not for a 26 inch bike. I also learned that I couldn't fly like Superman by jumping off the chicken house with a feed sack tied around my neck; even though my brother said I could. What a guy; he was my hero; I loved him dearly.

Once when I was about 4 or 5 my mother heard a racket out at the chicken pen which was right next to the hog pen and she discovered that one of her best laying hens had flown over the fence into the hog pen and the hogs were trying to get it. It was lodged between the hog trough and the fence and they couldn't quite reach it; yet. She went into the hog pen after her chicken and the hogs, being excited already, went after momma. My brother, who must have been 11 or 12, grabbed a 2X4 and beat the hogs off so she could get out of the pen. She got her chicken too. That scene is burned into my brain. I'm still afraid of hogs.

I never realized how hard Momma had to work to keep up with the place and us kids but she really enjoyed it. I don't think she knew how much until we moved away and she didn't have it anymore.

I went through the first and second grade in Union and as I recall I did pretty well. This was before the days of TV so for entertainment, Mother would read to the whole family or if the whole family wasn't available (Dad was working and my brother was in school) she would read to me and have me read to her. She taught me to read before I started school. Those are some more pleasant memories. I remember the age of four pretty vividly. I remember her doing the laundry out in the yard on a wringer washing machine once a week. I helped her anyway I could and I do remember it plainly so I must have been interested. I remember the smells of the bleach and the bluing. I remember the iron heating on the wood cook stove and a bottle with holes in the stopper that she used to sprinkle the clothes when she ironed them. Steam irons hadn't been invented.

There was a cellar under the house to store home canned veggies, and potatoes and other root crops in. She told me never to go down there "'cause there were vipers down there." There weren't 'cause she wouldn't have gone down there if there had been but it kept me out of the cellar anyway.

Most of the toys I had were either homemade or second hand. I don't think there even were a lot of toys available, not anything like today at least. For one thing, there wasn't plastic for toys. I had a cap gun once but lost it when we were picking huckleberries up in the Blue Mountains. I think it said Roy Rogers on it. My brother whittled two wooden pistols for me with his pocket knife and made holsters and a gun belt out of an old inner tube, I really liked them. I was interested in my mother's Kodak box camera too so she made one for me to play with out of a cardboard box, a couple of spools some red cellophane and various things she had around the house. It even had film with numbers on it. It was very believable.

Little blocks of wood became ships floating in a harbor; *irrigation ditch*, and pea pods minus the peas plus a toothpick or two made very descent canoes. I did have a tricycle and a red wagon, but I only remember those because of old pictures. I remember those wooden pistols and the box camera much better. Since there was no such thing as television I had a terrific imagination. When I got a little older I started playing with my brothers things, like his Red Ryder bb gun. By that time he was more interested in girls. I think he carried newspapers to get enough money to buy it. He also milked our two cows and he got some of the money for selling the milk.

Meanwhile, a few different companies had came up with gasoline powered chain saws to cut down trees with and my dad got in on the ground floor, so to speak, as he had gotten the opportunity to test one in the woods. He heard that there was a lot of money to be made in the south coast Oregon mountains cutting big old growth douglas fir trees down with these new chain saws. His older brother had just got out of the navy, so the two of them made a trip to check it out. They went to

Glendale Oregon, bought a house on a piece of property that also had a second house on it that was under construction for $3000.00. They got hired to go to work cutting timber, came back to Union and said "get packed, we're moving." Another Uncle from Idaho came up with a stake bed Ford farm truck and loaded all of our stuff in it and away we went. It was about 600 miles but it took about 3 days. We drove in the daytime and camped at night. I remember sleeping under the truck with the dog down by a river. I was 7. I would start the 3rd grade in the fall.

There were no freeways where we were going just 2 lane blacktop if we were lucky. We looked like a bunch of refuges for sure. Our car was a 37 ford coupe. My uncle had a 39 Lincoln Zepher 4 dr. with a V12 engine. He parked it in our front yard when we got there and I don't think it ever ran again. I remember at some point in time that it had a very healthy crop of mushrooms growing in the mohair upholstery in the back seat. I think he finally gave it to someone who came by and asked him for it. I do know that dad finally did the same thing with the 37 ford. Mother drove the 37 ford all over when we lived in Union but dad bought a 49 Mercury a couple of years after we moved and mother didn't like it and she quit driving.

Glendale was a sawmill town. I recall there were 4 sawmills there, each with its own wigwam burner belching wood smoke 24 hours a day. It was a beautiful little valley but the smoke was so thick you couldn't see it. Lumber carriers was a major part of the traffic in town as lumber was stacked down town across the street from the stores as if the town was just part of the mill yard. You could also hear the sawmill machinery screaming 24 hours a day. You got used to it.

A wigwam burner is a conical shaped steel structure about 40 feet tall and about 40 feet across the bottom and probably 30 feet across the top with a heavy screen on top that all sawmills used to have to burn sawdust and waste wood scraps.

Life was really different for mother after moving to Glendale. She had no critters to tend and care for other than the dog and of course us kids. She had no garden. The soil was red clay and a garden wouldn't grow in it. The road going by our house was a dirt road (as were most of the roads in and about town) and the dust would just billow when cars would go by. This made it a lesson in futility to hang clothes on the line, that and the sparks from the wigwam burner from the mill down at the corner burning holes in the clothes and the sheets. You also had to keep a sharp eye out for grass fires in the summer time.

After we had been there a short time dad started working for a company on the Oregon coast which meant that he had to stay in a boarding house during the week and just come home on weekends. He was so tired from working all week, when he came home, that he only wanted to rest. Momma was very lonely.

There were a couple of ladies in the neighborhood that asked her to join the Rebecca Lodge and she did, eventually attaining the office of Chaplin. She was however still lonesome for dad and she finally got him to join the Odd Fellows which is the men's branch of the same lodge. However, although he agreed to join, he never agreed to participate and he didn't. Dad was never a joiner. Consequently neither am I.

My mother gave birth to another baby boy when I was 16. That gave both of them something to love and helped their relationship with each other too.

Chapter Two: My Education.

❖❖❖❖

I started school in the 3rd grade in Glendale Oregon. Everyone there was a trans-plant from somewhere: Arkansas. Texas, Tennessee, Florida, Oklahoma, well you get the picture. I was a pretty big kid for my age so the other boys must have decided that I was a challenge. The first thing that I recall as something that would later become a problem was at recess one kid got down on his hands and knees behind me and another boy pushed me down over the first boy. Then they yelled "Dog pile", and about a dozen kids jumped on top of me. I guess panic set in 'cause I couldn't breathe and I gave some of them black eyes and bloody lips. The teacher, since I was new, and the kids told her it was my fault, gave me a spanking for fighting on the school grounds. Then she sent a note home to my mother telling her that I had to stop hurting those poor children and that I didn't know my own strength. The other kids thought that was pretty cool that they could go to the teacher and say "he hit me" even when I hadn't and the teacher would spank me. My brother was having the same troubles that I was but it was more serious since he was older. The principal told the lettermen to take a large wooden paddle and whip him and he refused to submit to it. They sent a note to my mother saying that he wouldn't let the lettermen discipline him and mother said that she would have been disappointed in him if he had. About a year or two later he got mixed up with a girl at school and got her pregnant. He quit school and got married when he was seventeen so then I was pretty much on my own. Actually though, he didn't protect me anyway except for some moral support. He had taught me how to protect myself from the time I was a baby practically and he thought I was big enough and tough enough to fight my own battles. He would say things like" the bigger they are the harder they fall." Once there was a kid that was several years older than I that was trying to pick a fight with me after school. My brother just happened to come along and I thought, alright, I'm saved, but no, instead my brother said that I was almost as big as that kid and I better whip him or he would whip me when we got home. I tied into him and got knocked on my behind about 3 times. I told my brother that I would stand a better chance whipping him than winning that fight. I then walked home and he never tried to whip me.

I never ever picked a fight or had a fight that I could walk away from but the school authorities wouldn't believe that. Nobody at school could whip me except the teachers so I was bullied all through school with the help of the teachers. I recall one incident in the sixth grade when we all came in from recess and all of the boys were thirsty from running and playing. The drinking fountain was across the hall from our room and there was a line of kids getting a drink before going inside. I was at the end of the line and just as it got to be my turn the teacher stepped into the hall way and said that was enough and for all of us to get into the room. I was so thirsty that I grabbed a quick mouthful of water before I went in and the teacher grabbed my arm, jerking me away from the fountain and slapped me across the face. He then told me to wait in the hall till he got the class settled and then he would deal with me. Needless to say I didn't wait for him to come back and finish what he had started, instead I went home and told my mother what had transpired and she sent my brother down to the school to tell the teacher that he was invited to our house to talk to my father that evening. He did come and I wasn't allowed to be present, so I don't know exactly what was said but he never hit me again. My schoolwork slipped into failing grades. Looking back now I didn't think anyone cared so I didn't care either. Dad was working away from home so I only saw him on weekends. I tried to tell him of the trouble I was having, and he in response would tell me how tough he had it when he was a boy. He told me that he and his brothers had to sleep in the barn with the horses and the mules but somehow I never got anything out of those conversations that I could use. When I tried to tell him that I was unhappy because I didn't have friends he told me that I didn't need friends. That he and mother and my brother were all the friends I needed and everybody else were just "acquaintances". Once he told me about a woman teacher that was going to whip him with a harness strap and that she drew back and said "God bless this strap" and he said God bless my fist" and he hit her and knocked her over the desk. Now let me see, are you telling me I should hit my teacher and knock him/her over the desk? *Yeah, I guess he was.*

By the time I got into high school I wouldn't go out of the house to games or any school function where I thought I might run into my antagonists by myself, however I did have a few friends who had been bullied also so we stuck together for protection. We were pretty tough so we weren't bothered usually as long as they couldn't catch us alone. However one night after a game we were walking home and a car load of them jumped us on an unlit road between school and town. By the time it was over we had soundly whipped three of them and threw the driver over the guard rail into the black berry briars below. Now these were not kids my own age. These were students that were as much as two grades ahead of me. As I said I was big for my age and I looked like I was as old as they were. The kids in my class hadn't bothered me since we were little, 3rd and 4th grade. I actually got along quite well with my own class mates and the kids that were younger.

I actually tried to fit in. I thought that maybe if I went out for sports with them and I showed them that I actually had some talent that they might accept me as an equal. So I went out for football at the beginning of my sophomore year and several of my antagonists jumped me the first chance they had and stomped me pretty good while the coach watched. I talked to Dad about it and he told me to "fill a sock full of nuts and bolts and beat their damn brains out with it." Wow. (The *charge is first degree premeditated murder with a weapon. How do you plea?)*

I remember one day at lunch time I was in the hall to get a book from my locker. Suddenly I had about six people crowded around me. They were punching me and slamming my head against the locker. A teacher who was also the counselor walked by and we made eye contact and he just kept walking. They stopped when he walked by though, enough that I could break free and run into an empty class room. They followed me in and I picked up a chair to defend myself with, but luckily, a friend who had graduated the year before walked in and said "What the hell is going on in here?" and kids scattered. I don't remember why he came to the school that day but I'm glad he did.

I finally convinced dad that I needed to do something different so I was enrolled in school in Grants Pass High School for my Junior year. I had to drive to Wolf Creek, about seven miles, to catch the school bus and one morning I was distracted by a pop bottle rolling around in the floor boards of the pickup before I even got out of town and I drove right into a light pole. Since seat belts didn't exist in those days I whacked the windshield pretty hard with my head. I drove my 49 ford, that my brother had given me, to catch the school bus the rest of the year. I enjoyed going to school in Grants Pass but it was pretty expensive with tuition and other expenses, so in the fall of 59 I intended to start my senior year in Glendale. I would have probably done well because I wouldn't have had upper class men to distract me, but I was told I couldn't start my classes until I spoke with the Superintendent. After sitting in a chair in the hall way all morning the superintendent finally called me into his office about lunch time and told me that he didn't want my kind in his school. I told him I didn't much want to be there either so I left. A month later I turned 17 and joined the navy.

I needed some money to get by on before I went into the navy though, and I managed to get a Job in a saw mill in the neighboring town of Wolf Creek. One morning as I walked out to my car to go to work, I never got there. Dad was home for whatever reason and he heard a racket outside and came out to see what the problem was. He found me on the ground in convulsions. He carried me in to the house and called the town Dr. The Dr come to the house and after examining me said he didn't know what it was but that it wasn't epilepsy. *How did he know that?* So I got out of bed and went to work and made some excuse why I was late.

When I filled out my paperwork to join the navy they asked me if I'd ever had a seizure. I said no. I spent several years in denial concerning this. It didn't fit into my self image. It actually stemmed from the car accident I had when I ran into the pole on the way to school but no one figured that out including a prominent neurologist even though he had all of the information. It took a Chiropractor to figure this out and fix it in about 1986.

On Jan 11 1960, I took a bus to Portland Oregon and a new adventure. I took care of my swearing in duties and left Portland the next day in a snow storm. When we circled San Diego, coming in for a landing, I could see blue sky, blue water and palm trees. I thought: wow, this is going to be fun. I had no way of knowing what was in store for me.

We landed at the airport in San Diego. The air had smells that I had never smelled at home, Sea Gulls were screaming, and a warm breeze was blowing. A long grey school bus picked us up and took us out to Naval Training Center.

When we got off the bus we were told to stand at attention and were yelled at until we got the idea. Then we got all of our hair cut off. Then we were issued clothes that fit poorly and shoes that we would learn to spit shine. Then we were marched to the barracks that we were informed would be our home for the next 9 weeks. We were taught to march. Some of us were better at this than others. We were made to memorize something called "General Orders." We were taught to handle a rifle. That is to do a rifle manual. *It's kind of like twirling a baton only with a rifle.* We actually fired a rifle at the range one time. They didn't put as much emphasis on small arms training in the Navy as they did in the Marines and the Army. We were taught to shine shoes and belt buckles. Everything seemed to be pretty much for show. We also learned how to wash our clothes with a bucket of water on a concrete table with a little brush and a bar of soap and how to hang them on a line with little pieces of string called clothes stops, and being sure to tie them on with a square knot. Woe be to the recruit that hangs his socks up with a granny Knot. And don't forget and call your "rifle " your "gun" or you would find yourself standing in the middle of the barracks floor in your underwear,(skivvies) with your "rifle" in one hand and your crotch in the other reciting: "THIS IS MY RIFLE AND THIS IS MY GUN, THIS IS FOR FIGHTING AND THIS IS FOR FUN!" I think the main thing that we were supposed to learn was team work and discipline and how to follow orders. I think I must have missed some of those classes.

Chapter Three: When I Left Home

◇◇◇◇

When I left home (for the first time in my life) I was bringing some baggage with me from my school days. I had spent so much time trying to keep from getting in fights in school ('cause I lost even when I won) that I had begun to think that I was a coward and I didn't like myself very well, so I had made up my mind that I would never run from a fight again. The very worse decision I made however was to stop listening to my "gut feeling" that told me when to walk away and when to run. I still knew the difference between right and wrong but I would choose to ignore it. Bad idea!

I made it through boot camp without too much difficulty although at the time I thought that my CO was picking on me because he wouldn't consider me for any of the recruit petty officer duties. Just another case, I thought, of being picked last for the team. After all, I thought, I have the ability to do what is required. I believe now though that it was because I was a high school dropout. That does not usually show much leadership potential, but at the time I was looking for someone else to blame for it.

After boot camp I was assigned to the USS Sperry. AS12. A submarine tender based at San Diego, but first I had to deal with about 14 days of Leave. So I took a Grey Hound bus back to my home town. Nothing much had changed except the girls thought I looked cute in my uniform, And Dad had sold my car so I got to use his. I managed to ding the front fender up before I left so my brother found a body shop to fix it and I left town before dad found out about it. (Now that was brave wasn't it?)

I reported to duty aboard ship around the 1st of April 1960. About the time that I would have been graduating had I stayed in high school. I took a water taxi out to the ship that was anchored in San Diego bay along with her sister ship, The USS Nereus. AS 17. I was assigned a "rack" (navy for bed) and a locker in the R- 1 division, but before I could get to working on submarines I would have to put in my time working on the mess decks, banging out stainless trays in a garbage can. The trays were actually washed in a dishwasher. Then I learned how to use a mop, and how to polish brass, painting, cleaning, and waxing floors. (decks) But I had Lots of liberty and I had a cousin, 21 years old, who lived in San Diego who I enjoyed visiting. He was married with a small baby and he lived with his wife and Grand Parents who had raised him. However, he had been diagnosed with Hodgkin's disease and at that time it was considered terminal. He was pretty upbeat though. He was taking flying lessons and doing all kinds of fun things. It was hard to believe he was really dying. He never talked about it. Maybe he was in denial but It was nice to have family to visit with when I was away from home.

One weekend though, (what was I thinking) I just decided to go home. I had gotten paid so I went to the locker club, got into my civies and hopped a bus for Oregon. While I was gone the ship went to Long Beach so I missed ships movement. I was court martialed and spent 30 days in the brig at the naval station. Now that wasn't really fun but when I look back on it though it was an adventure. It was also dangerous and I thrived on danger back then, maybe to prove to myself that I wasn't afraid, or maybe because I didn't have better sense. After I was there a few days they put me (and some others) on an outside work detail making fenders for ships out of rope. The guard (Shore Patrol) was a nut job and he talked to me all the time we were marching to where the work was (about a mile as I recall) and tried to talk me into running. "Go ahead" he said "I won't shoot you." Somehow I never believed him.

When I went back aboard ship I was working in the Repair-1 Div. and that was kind of fun. They never gave me anything too critical to work on, as I was still in training, but I always tried to do a good job of what I did do. They had lost their Yeoman for the division through a transfer so after awhile, I was assigned to that. I met another div. yeoman and became friends with him. He had a girlfriend in Texas and she had a sister so we became pen pals and started writing letters back and forth. One day while my new friend and I were on liberty we saw a 51 ford convert at a gas station for sale. The guy wanted 25 dollars for it, because he said it had a blown head gasket. So we pooled our resources and bought it as I knew I could fix it. One day the next week after I had put a new gasket on it, I was driving through San Diego and turned left from the wrong lane and got stopped. That sounds pretty simple but I had to go to court a week later and since I had no money to pay a fine the Judge gave me a week in jail. When I got back to the ship they tossed me in the ships brig for being AWOL. again. While I was in the ships brig I had a grand mal seizure. The next thing I knew I was in Balboa Naval Hospital.

I was pretty upset that I had had another seizure. I was still in denial that I really had anything wrong with me. They tried everything they could come up with to trigger another episode but they could not. They rigged me up with flashing lights and bells and all kinds of things while I was wired up with EEG equipment to monitor brain waves. Then it was like they forgot about me. No one communicated anything to me about anything so I had no Idea really what their plans were for me. I had a bed to sleep in. I received a pay envelope once a month. I had a permanent liberty Pass. I could come and go as I pleased. I was pretty much on track to get a medical discharge I thought, with some kind of disability pay. Then I met Denny.

Denny was about 19 I think. He was from Montana. He had a car, a 53 Buick 2 door hard top. I don't know what he was doing in the hospital however I do know that he was a serial liar and an absolute criminal. I didn't pick up on the liar part of it right away but the criminal part made him seem dangerous and interesting so we became friends. Denny parked his car on base at the Hospital and I think it may have had an Officer or a Dr's sticker on the license plate or something as he would set in the back seat and I drove in uniform as we were leaving the main gate. We would not even have to stop and the duty officer would snap to attention and salute us as we went out the gate.

He always seemed to have money and I never knew where he got it. I know he told me once that his daddy was rich and he sent him all this money, but Denny told me a lot of things and that particular thing turned out to be a lie. We went to San Bernardino once. We ran all over the San Diego area. He introduced me to some civilians that he knew. One of them had a house at La Jolla cove. We would climb down a trail in his back yard and dive for lobster. We called it going "bug hunting." We would bring them up to his house and cook them on his barbecue. We even went to Mexico a few times. We could drink and party down there. He had a fake ID that he could buy beer with on this side of the border too so we did drink some beer when we were running around.

He had been on a ship that was stationed in Long Beach so one day we decided to go to long Beach to visit some of his Shipmates. There was an amusement park in Long Beach known as the Pike. We met his friends and walked around there for several hours flirting with girls, and basically just hanging out. Somebody (probably Denny) suggested that we should go roll a queer. Now I had never even thought of doing anything like that but I wasn't about to say I was scared (even if I was). At first it looked like it wasn't really going to happen. There was a loop there by the Pike where the Homos would cruise around and around the loop hoping to pick up some young sailor away from home and lonesome. The plan was that one of us would go stand on the street corner and allow ourselves to get picked up and the others would follow until the person in the car with the queer started something then we would pull him out of the car and rob him. One of Denny's buddy's went and stood on the corner for about an hour and had no takers. I thought that would be that but no, they thought I should try my luck because, they said I was "younger and pinker" Of course I couldn't let them know that I was scared to death so I went over to the street corner and the first car that came by stopped. A brand new white 1960 Studebaker Lark. "Get in, "the guy said. "Where are you going'?" "Back to San Diego" I said. He said he would take me. Then he said "I've been out fucking around, would you like to fuck around with me." I really didn't think I could carry through with this up till that moment. I had never hurt anybody that wasn't trying to hurt me and I had never stolen anything. That went against my personal moral code. He had driven to a dark secluded residential area and as he stopped at a stop sign he reached down and put his hand on my thigh. I turned and hit him in the ear with my fist as hard as I could. The Buick drove up behind us, someone jerked the door open he fell out on the ground. He appeared to be out cold. Denny grabbed his wallet the other guys jumped into the Studebaker and took off and we jumped into the Buick and we were gone too. The whole thing couldn't have taken more than thirty seconds. Denny said the guy wouldn't report it to the police and he might not have if they hadn't stolen his new car and, I found out later, ran it into the ocean.

We went back to San Diego as fast as that Buick would take us. We didn't hear anything about it so we thought we were in the clear but Denny made the mistake of not throwing away the man's wallet. We went down to Mexico and partied for a few days I think there was a couple of hundred dollars in the wallet and that was a lot back then. We came back to the states and as we were driving through San Diego we were stopped. When they searched the car they found the wallet under the seat complete with the man's drivers license. I didn't even know it was there. Next stop LA County Jail.

LA County Jail. Now that was different. Denny and I were separated and we both signed a confession. No sense in lying.

We were caught. We were put in separate cell blocks for several days before we were sentenced. There were only a couple of things that I really remember from that particular episode. One day I walked down through the cell block just for something to do and I observed a couple of black men in a cell with a young white boy, *about my age,* and they were attempting to rape him. He was crying but not fighting much 'cause he was too scared. I walked on down the tier and told a couple of white men what was happening thinking I could get some help, and they told me to mind my own business or I might get hurt. I didn't think I could look in the mirror if I did so I went back up to the cell where it was going on, I stopped and said "Turn him loose sunshine". They were totally shocked and they loosed their hold on the kid and he squirted out the door. One of them stood up and said "What did you call me whitey"? I said "Sunshine". He caught me in the jaw with a punch that I didn't even see coming. Then he turned and walked back in his cell. I felt like my jaw was dislocated for days. I felt good about myself though. I also learned that I couldn't expect help from anyone else there. Everyone in the cell block knew what was going on but wouldn't do anything to stop it. The kid went and hid in his cell and didn't even say thank you. However I saw the black guys a few times after that and they treated me with respect. That was a lesson learned also.

A few days later we were sentenced to a year in LA County Jail and one year probation and since I was a Juvenile the crime and the sentence would be erased from my record after I had done my time and completed my probation. The Judge recommended that we serve our time at a facility called Wayside Honor Rancho. It was a minimum security prison complex surrounded by chainlink with razor wire on the top.

The day we were to be transferred a bunch of us were put in a small room, probably 16 foot square with no windows or ventilation. There were probably 25 or 30 of us in that room. There was one large solid door about 4 inches thick with a lock that took a huge key like an old skeleton key. It was very hot in that room and we were rapidly running out of oxygen. I laid down on the floor with my face next to the door and I could feel a little cool air coming under the door. I really thought we were going to die in there. For some reason I had a nylon rat tail comb in my pocket. I have no idea why they hadn't taken it away from me. After about an hour in there I used that comb to pick that lock and open that door a few inches. No one came to check on us for some time, probably another hour anyway. The guard that came to get us for our transfer was really mad that the door was unlocked but of course he didn't know that I had done it. He thought it was an accident. We would have died in there if I hadn't been able to get that door open. Next stop: Wayside Honor Rancho.

It was way better than the county jail in LA. We were in a dorm with pretty good beds and decent food, and tables where we ate and played cards and dominoes. If you had money you could buy things: cigarettes, candy and toiletries. After I was there for about a week I decided I wanted something to do so they gave me a job of walking up and down the hall pushing a dust mop. There were several dorms and they had heavy glass windows so that the guards could see into them when they were walking down the hall way. As I was walking down that hall one day I observed in one of the dorms several quite attractive young women bare from the waist up with large breasts and boxer shorts on the bottom. I could hardly believe what I was seeing. Then I really got a shock. When they saw me looking at them one of them dropped her shorts. Or should I say his shorts. I had heard about such but I had never seen anything like that before. The rest of my stay there was pretty uneventful and I was released early for good behavior. I had been discharged from the navy while I was in there and the Judge said I could return to Oregon to finish my probation, so after making my way back to downtown L.A. it was back on a Grey Hound and headed back to Oregon. Of course it wasn't California's fault but I had had all of California that I wanted for the foreseeable future. Dad picked me up at the bus depot and took me to work with him in the woods for the rest of the week. I don't think he felt he could trust me out of his sight. Who could blame him? However, I enjoyed being with dad. And I could always learn things from him when I was working with him.

By then I was 18 and old enough to go to work in the woods or the mills. I chose the woods and didn't have any trouble getting a high lead choker setting job. Dad still had the 1952 ford pickup that he let me drive until I got something of my own. I got a couple of cars but they were broke down a lot so I drove that pickup a lot. A friend of mine, that I had gone to school with, and I went down to the local lunch counter one day where I met my future wife. We took her and her girlfriend out that night in that old pickup. We parked, drank some beer and her and I really hit it off. I had never been in love with anyone before but before long I was absolutely crazy about her. I couldn't stay away from her. I'm sure her parents got sick of having me around. We weren't having sex at that point but I was absolutely smitten. I think she was 16 and I was 18. We went together for probably 18 months. I was I believe 20 when we got married and she was 18. She got pregnant. We got married and Things went down hill after that. I had a couple of seizures, I couldn't work in the woods anymore. We made an appointment with a Neurologist and He checked me out. He gave me a spinal tap and I was in the hospital In Medford when my dad took my wife to the hospital in Canyonville to have our baby.

The Dr. had my drivers license taken away for a year, supposedly till my seizure problem was controlled. However since I had never been too good at following rules I was still driving. I got caught driving and the state took it away for another year. The charge was driving while suspended. I continued to drive but one night after my wife and I had had a fight over her sister using my car when I had told her not to, I went out with some of my friends and I wrecked the car. So then we didn't even have a car. Times were really tough back then. Worse than they are now I think. There were no Jobs doing anything. The unemployment office was packed every day. The state came up with a program that they would send you to a trade school and support you and your family with welfare money if you qualified. I applied for it and was accepted, and I decided I wanted to be a body and fender man. So they paid to move us to Eugene Oregon, rented an apt. and enrolled me in Eugene Technical Vocational School. So I was back in school again. No car no transportation except walking. Couldn't even afford cigarettes and we both smoked. I think cigarettes cost a whole $2.00 a carton then. She didn't like welfare and being broke any better than I did and I'm sure she started asking herself, what did I ever marry this loser for? I was still crazy in love with her but I don't think she even liked me anymore.

I started looking around and I found a part time job

working in a gas station. About 2 weeks later I was at work one Saturday and who should show up but Denny. He had called my folks looking for me and lied about who he was so that they told him. I asked him how he had found me and he told me. That should have been a clue that he hadn't changed. He was still good at telling lies. He was living in Portland, married with a couple of kids, had a nice house and wanted us to stay with them for a few days. It sounded like a vacation to us after what we had been doing so we went. I hoped that he had mended his ways and got his life back on track. Well, not so you could notice. It turned out he was a serial burglar and shoplifter, pimp and God only knows what else. When they got really hard up his wife would go out and turn tricks. When I found out which way the wind was blowing, I extracted my wife, our baby, and myself from that mess and went back to Eugene. It was probably the first smart thing that I ever did concerning Denny.

When we got back our daughter who then was about a year old had an asthma attack and I had to rush her to the hospital. When I got home we had a fight because she absolutely refused to go get her driver license, (although she still wanted to drive the car) so we could go places without my losing my license for yet another year. I had a car then, a 56 Pontiac that I had bought on credit after going to work in the gas station. I went to the Hospital the next day to see my baby and she was in an oxygen tent. I put my hand in and she grabbed my finger and smiled at me. The next day I went to the hospital to see her and she wasn't there. My wife and her mother had taken her. I saw her once after that then never saw her again till she was 14.

I went back to a motel room that I had rented, checked out and went back to Southern Oregon and got a job driving a fork lift in the plywood mill. I called my wife and went to see her and my daughter and I told her I had a pretty good job and asked her to come home with me and she refused. She said she loved me but she couldn't live with me. I do understand. I even did then.

I continued to work and was doing pretty good at my job. I had bought a Ford pickup for transportation to get back and forth to work as the Pontiac had blown the motor. One evening I decided to drive down town. I still didn't have a license but I knew the cops in town and they hadn't stopped me before while going to and from work so I wasn't worried. I got stopped and I got a ticket for no license and that meant I would lose my license for yet another year. Well, here comes another bad idea. Rather than go to court and take my medicine, I quit my job and left town. I went to Idaho where my Grandparents lived. I had very little money, feeling sorry for myself and drinking heavy, a recipe for disaster. I did try to find a job but I could find nothing. My cousin, a 15 year old girl had got the Idea she wanted to run away with me and I guess she had delusions of us being a modern day Bonny and Clyde. She stole a gun from her mother and gave it to me which I dropped in my jacket pocket. I was drinking down at the local pub one night and ran out of money before I ran out of thirst. I drove across the border into Oregon and robbed a motel. Two days later I was in jail in Vale Oregon. I was a very inept criminal.

A few days later I was arraigned on the charge of first degree armed robbery. Even I could figure out that was liable to carry some heavy time with it, so I tried to lie my way out of it. I plead not guilty and told my Court appointed attorney that I did not remember any of it. That I had epilepsy and that I must have blacked out or something. That probably wasn't a very good Idea as If I had gotten away with the charade I probably would have been stuck in the state mental hospital for who knows how long. So the next thing I knew I was off to Eastern Oregon State Hospital for evaluation.

There were some of the strangest people in there. Probably the strangest ones were the orderlies. One of them thought it was cool to shuffle his feet on a carpeted floor and build up a static charge then put his finger next to some ones ear. He did it to several people, me included. It really hurt but he thought it was very funny. There was one person who he did it to who was being evaluated before sentencing for murder. I was playing cards with him at the time and he was so startled that he upset the card table. The orderly thought that was the funniest thing he had ever seen. The man calmly told him, not to do that again. He set the table back up and we resumed our game. The next day he did it again and the orderly went out of there on a stretcher.

Then there was a young boy in there. He was probably ten. I know most in this day and age will find this hard to believe but in 1964 the State Hospitals were the dumping ground for any one that the state found themselves stuck with and didn't know what else to do with them. The story was that the boy and his sister, who was a year younger than him were at home with a babysitter one night when their parents went out to dinner. At the time the children were six and seven. The parents were involved in a fatal car crash on the way home. With the parents both dead the children had no living relatives. There were no orphanages in Oregon and the State Hospital was as close as you got to one. I don't think they had a foster parent program then either. Twice a day they medicated us with thorazine to keep us mellow. It was mandatory. Yes, the boy too. About every 2 hours they gave us a cigarette, and lit it for us as we couldn't have matches. Yes, the boy too. Every once in a while I could hear the most God awful screams. I was told it was someone who they had decided was violent or incorrigible having electro shock therapy. I was glad I was just there for evaluation.

The Drs there were pretty good and probably did the most thorough examination of me that I had had done to me to date. I was wired up every day. 5 days a week for about two weeks. I didn't know what they had found out at the time except they changed and increased my medication. I was there for 30 days then they returned me to Vale and the Malheur county jail. All told I was incarcerated in one place or another for almost five months before I went to trial.

The Dr. from the hospital was my star witness, although the DA, thought he was going to be the States star witness. They (the state) put him on the witness stand and he said that with the type of epilepsy that I had that I could have had a psycho-motor episode in which case I wouldn't be responsible for committing the crime. Needless to say neither the DA nor the Judge wanted to hear that and when the case went to the Jury they couldn't reach a verdict so the Judge had to declare it a hung jury and a mistrial. That however didn't mean I could go home, just that they would get a do over. So back to Jail I went for another month or so then my dad, probably against his better judgment, but at my mother's insistence, bailed me out with a stipulation by the court that I would have to go into the State Hospital one more time for another evaluation, only this time at Salem. It turned out that they had actually fired that other Dr. from the state hospital because of his testimony and they wanted someone on their side on the witness stand.

So, about a month or so later I found myself at the Western Oregon State Hospital. Wow, what adventures I was having.

This wasn't as bad as the other place was at least from my point of view. Since I was free on bail, or at least I wasn't locked up. No one was drugging me with Thorazine or rationing my cigarettes. As a matter of fact no one was doing anything to me. I was there for a month, and met a lot of people. I even ran into an old girl friend of mine. *She was a friend from high school who happened to be a girl.* I still don't know what happened to her for sure. She had been a very sharp, bright attractive girl and now she didn't even recognize me. She had hair two inches long growing on her legs, and had an ugly old bath robe on and all she could say was "gimmie a cigarette." I worked on one of the wards for about two weeks for something to do before they let me go home and I was abhorred at the way the patients were treated. There was a patient who thought that a male orderly was his wife when he was feeding him his lunch and reached out and stroked his face. The orderly shoved the tray into his face and ground it in. Another time I was walking through the ward and a man called out to me. I went to his bed and found him tied to his bed with restraints. He appeared to be intelligent and articulate. He was also an ex prize fighter. He told me that his Dr. had sent him there to be evaluated before putting him in a state run nursing home as he was destitute and couldn't pay for a regular nursing home and his arthritis was so bad that he couldn't take care of himself anymore. He guessed this must be the nursing home they were referring to because they kept him. He said the worst thing was the orderlies kept him tied to his bed and wouldn't even let him up to go to the bath room. I tried to check on it but could get no information. But the next day I was on the ward and I heard a commotion and found two orderlies cleaning the old man up after he had messed the bed. He was cussing those two with everything he could come up with. One of them took the rag that he had been wiping the bed with and stuffed it in the old mans mouth. I lost it. I went over and took the rag out of his mouth. Grabbed a rag out of the wash pan with some decidedly brown stain on it and stuffed it in the orderly's mouth. I can still hear the old man laughing. HE HE HE HE HE HE". I went home the next day without ever having had an EEG or any other tests.

About two months later I went back to court and was convicted in about two days. That Dr. lied and said he had given me a thorough evaluation and that I didn't have anything wrong with me. I used to see him often as he used to bring medications over to the prison and dispense it. He acted like he didn't know me. I shouldn't wonder. I don't recall the public defender saying anything during the whole trial. Real world court rooms are not like Matlock on television. I had it coming and I was guilty but I learned that if they want to convict someone of something they will one way or another. If they don't have the evidence, they will invent it. There are innocent men in prison. The Judge sentenced me to fifteen years and two days later I was heading for Salem Oregon and the Joint in the back seat of a police cruiser in shackles. At that time I don't think that reality had really set in. I think I was still just having a wild adventure. Reality would come.

They booked me in gave me clothes to wear , a kit with a razor, tooth brush, tooth powder, a plastic comb, a bar of soap a sack of Bull Durham and some rolling papers and a book of matches. Then they took me to someplace that they called A-Block. I thought wow, this isn't so bad. It was a room about 12 foot square that had a table and a seat (metal) hinged to the painted steel wall. Across the room a single bunk was hinged to the other wall. There was a stainless toilet and a stainless sink that had a feature so you could also use it for a drinking fountain. It was clean, well lit and no bars. This was called A Block. That was just where they put you when you first came in.

Chapter Four: The Joint

◇◇◇◇

After about 3 days they transferred me to D Block. It was 3 tiers high which amounts to 3 stories So with the first floor there were 4 levels of cells. I was put on the ground floor maybe because of my epilepsy, or maybe they just put me where they had space. There was about 20 feet from the front of the cells to the outside wall and the wall had windows with bars all the way to the top. The cells were numbered D101 D102 etc. There was a barber chair in front of D101. That's where the barber lived. I had some money in my account but I found out I could only go to the store once a week, I think on Friday and I believe this was Wednesday. I needed some things, like cigarettes and whatever to make life a little more livable. The barber seemed like a nice guy. He was a big black man. He offered to loan me some cigarettes . I promised to pay him back Saturday. He said "You better" and that was all he said.

The next day I got to go out to the exercise yard and I met a few people. During the course of our conversation I mentioned that I had borrowed cigarettes from this guy and what he had said. The fellow that I was talking to told me that the barber was a loan shark and that Prisoners used cigarettes for money in the joint and whatever I had borrowed I would be expected to pay it back four fold. They said that this guy does this with young men when they come in and they attempt to pay him back a carton of cigarettes for a carton of cigarettes and they get either beat up or forced to have sex with him or both. He had tried to make me take a carton but I'd only taken a couple of packs, mainly 'cause I didn't like the brand and I figured they would last until I could make it to the store to buy my brand. Camels were the preferred money brand and that was what he loaned me. Friday, I bought him a carton of Camels and myself two cartons of Pall Malls. He seemed disappointed.

This was a whole different culture and if I was going to survive I had a lot to learn and fast. Rule number 1. You don't talk to guards. You just say yes sir and no sir. If you do more than that the other cons will think you are a snitch. Number 2: you don't snitch (see number 1) number 3: Mind your own business (do your own time.) Number 4: Keep your mouth shut and your ears open but don't let anyone know you have your ears open. Sometimes people get killed for what they know. You need to try not to appear frightened and vulnerable. If you do they, *the other cons,* will use it against you. You mustn't show any weakness but don't act tough because you are not. You just keep learning from day to day, you must, it's a matter of survival.

The first day when I went to lunch I left the mess hall with that old familiar knot in the pit of my stomach. It was that old feeling that I used to associate with fear only this time it was saying to me: 'Now this could be dangerous, you had better pay attention if you want to survive this mess that you have gotten yourself into.' The mess hall was a long narrow room with two rows of long tables set crosswise the length of the room. On the opposite end that you came in on there were serving tables across the end. You stood in line without talking on the right and the left sides of the room. You did not talk while you were in the mess hall. There was an elevated screened in walk way around the top of the room with one or two guards patrolling around it with shotguns. A couple of days later I was in there and someone walked up behind another con in line and stuck a shank, *a homemade knife,* in him. Don't know why, never asked. Good not to know. Probably for snitching.

I sat in my cell for a few days and decided I needed a job. On checking what was available I thought I would like to work in the hospital. I had had some experience along those lines but nothing really close to this. However, I applied for it and I was given whites to wear and a schedule. I saw things in there that I wouldn't have believed. There was a con working in the hospital that I think either was a Dr. on the outside or he just had some serious medical training. No matter, every one called him Doc. A real Dr came in about once a week, meanwhile it was pretty much up to us to take care of a prison population of 2000 with what we had, basically volunteer undertrained inmates. It was up to us to sew up cuts, bandage scrapes give shots and even set broken bones. Sometimes the Dr. would show up but not always.

Doc and I were working together one evening and a con, probably in his mid 40s, came up complaining of chest pains. Suddenly he collapsed on the floor and Doc and I put him on a table and started working on him. We would get a heart beat then we'd lose it. Finally Doc gave him a shot of a heart stimulant drug in the heart. But we couldn't bring him back.

Defibrillators weren't invented at that time I don't think. We didn't have one anyway. Doc sat down next to the table and cried. We had been working on the guy for 4 and one half hours. The guard who was assigned to the hospital was in his office playing solitaire. He didn't seem too concerned.

Doc quit the hospital after that. I think he went to work in the laundry. Another time the guards brought a man up and put him in a padded cell in the hospital. He seemed perfectly normal and docile but they insisted we put him in a straight jacket. They left him there and sometime later I heard him start making sounds almost like a wounded bear. Moaning and growling and howling is the best I can describe it. Then suddenly he bowed his shoulders and the seams in that strait jacket popped wide open. The next thing I knew the strait jacket was lying on the floor. Then he simply lay down on the padded floor and went to sleep. The next day he went back to his cell in the cell block. I never did find out what that was about.

The inmates were pretty diverse as to what they had been before they were sent to prison. I had two teeth pulled while I was in there by a con that worked there. He had been a dentist on the outside. However he didn't have access to ex rays and anesthesia in there but he got the job done and it wasn't too bad. I had a tooth ache and didn't want to wait a week or so until an outside dentist would come in, so I asked him to take care of it. I worked there about a year and decided I didn't want to make a career out of it.

I had a chance to go to school and get my GED so I decided to do that. After I got my GED I decided that this might be a pretty good place to work. I was pretty good at typing and I remembered the way I had been taught to type in high school so I become the typing teacher. They had auto shop classes there also and they were teaching men how to work on automatic transmissions. Ford motor co. had just come out with a new type of automatic transmission. After manufacturing Ford-a-matic and Merc-a-matic transmissions for years they had developed a C-6 and a C-4. They gave me and some of my students the job of transposing a factory book on C-6 ford transmissions on mimeograph paper so that books could be duplicated for the auto shop students. We had a couple of artists who illustrated it. It took us about a month as I remember. Things were really different then. No computers, no scanners, no fax machines, no printers. I remember sometime while I was in there probably about 1968 they first started talking publically about Lasers. I first read about them in a Popular Science magazine. There was some speculation about the eventual use of them but as I recall, they didn't even scratch the surface. Wow it's hard to believe things have changed so much. It seems like a different world. Now I've heard them talking about some scheme where inmates are buying cell phones from the guards and using them someway in an illegal enterprise of some kind. They didn't even have cell phones in 1968.

There were other classes available with college credits and since I was in the school all day anyway I thought I should try and improve my resume as much as possible while I was in there One of the classes I opted to take was French, It was a popular class as the teacher was young, female and cute. However, no matter how hard I tried, I never seemed to quite get the hang of it. Maybe I was paying more attention to the teacher than the language or maybe I just wasn't cut out to be bilingual. I took creative writing which I enjoyed. I wrote some poetry and found I had a flair for it (who would have thought it?) I studied poetry and learned all about Stanza's and such things. However I don't think my creative writing teacher was too bright as I wrote a report on the Constitution and the concept of *"Separation of Church and State."* Which I had read about and researched from books I had found in the library. He gave me a failing grade because he said I should have written *"The Separation of THE Church and THE State.*

We had a group therapy session one night at the school and I signed up for it. I'd sign up for anything to get out of that cell. They said we should turn to the guy to our right and tell him what you really thought of him. The guy to my left was a guy that I had taken poetry classes with and I thought he liked me. He turned to me and told me that he thought I was a smart assed son of a bitch. I almost fell out of my chair. He then told me and the group that a few days previously at school he had complimented me on something I'd written and tried to ask me some questions concerning the mechanics of poetry and I hadn't responded, which embarrassed him. The reason that I had blew him off is that I wasn't used to compliments and I had an inferiority complex. The teacher recognized this and explained that bashful people are often misread this way. Since then I've always tried to pay attention when anyone talks to me and acknowledge them. It was a good lesson. I told him I was sorry I'd ignored him and he said he was sorry he called me a son of a bitch.

The most important class and the one which had the biggest impact on my life though, wasn't really a class at all. It was more like group therapy mixed with a church service. They offered a weekly alcoholics anonymous meeting Tuesday nights in the mess hall. I didn't consider myself an alcoholic but, it was better than setting in a cell all night, right? So I went, and I listened and I learned and I found myself giving a testimony and saying I was an alcoholic, a few nights later, after I learned what an alcoholic really was. I learned that it wasn't just someone who slept under a bridge with a wine bottle, but rather someone who has trouble with judgment while drinking and is unable or unwilling to admit it and stop doing it. I learned that most of my trouble wouldn't have happened if I had been sober. For me however, the most important thing I learned was the alcoholic's motto: "I AM RESPONSIBLE". The booze wasn't responsible. I was responsible. It was my fault, and no one else's. That was a new concept for me and also would have been for most if not all of the men in that prison. That is something that should be drummed into all men and women that find themselves in a similar situation. I believe it would make a difference. For me though, It really felt good to reach that conclusion because that meant I could actually do something about my life to change simply by being responsible. There was power in that simple motto. That was when I stopped blaming everybody else for everything that had happened to me. That night in my cell I also asked Jesus Christ to take control of my life. I didn't know at the time if he had heard me because I didn't have any religious training but things seemed to go better for me after that. I really started to think I was going to be ok. I continued to go to AA meetings and I really enjoyed it. I think the reason I did was that It was nice to be in the company of men who were really interested in turning their lives around. So many were constantly scheming something new to get into when they got out. Funny thing though, several of the men in AA were lifers and would never get out. Sometimes you really just have to make the best of what you have. Acting responsibly is a good thing no matter where you are. I went to church a few times but didn't get the same feeling that I did from AA. It seemed that some of the men going to church were using it as a means to an end. Not because they believed it, but because they wanted someone else to believe they believed it. (like the parole board for instance.) At that point in time Christianity was considered a good thing. No one knew anything about Muslims. There was a country western song out then though. It was a total spoof called *Ahab the Arab*. That would probably get your head cut off these days.

Christianity is not easy. It takes study to understand it and if you don't understand it you can't believe it or you wind up simply confused not knowing what you believe. There is much more to it than saying "I am a Christian." I liked the concept of it and I definitely liked the idea of my sins being forgiven but it would be years before I would be able to say with confidence that I was saved and that I was a born again Christian.

Chapter Five:
Western State Hospital – Again

❖❖❖❖

I had a problem that I couldn't seem to get past. I continued to have seizures. Sometimes overexertion would bring one on. I enjoyed playing hand ball and sometimes after a game I would wake up in the hospital. Sometimes I would have one at breakfast while drinking my coffee. There seemed to be no set pattern or definite trigger. Someone at the prison, possibly the prison physician who testified against me in court, decided they needed to send me over to the state hospital next door and have me evaluated in a controlled environment. So I was packed up and moved once again to Oregon state hospital. Only this time I was moved onto a maximum security ward with lots of locked doors to go through. In short it was a ward for the criminally insane. The first day I was there I thought I might have a problem. I was already taking Dilantin which is an anticonvulsant and phenobarbitol which is a narcotic. Then they added something called Tridione. I had been taking the first two of these things for quite some time and was acclimated so to speak and the third one wasn't real noticeable at first in the way it made me feel. It smelled like coconut. But then here came that damn Thorazine. I knew what that damn stuff was and I had enough of my wits about me to realize that maybe that particular cocktail might kill me. But that is just what the orderlies on those wards did to everyone in order to more easily control them and they were not about to make an exception for me. They had started using that drug in 1954 to control patients in institutions and it has been likened to a "chemical lobotomy." When I had been in the Eastern Oregon State Hospital years earlier they had given it as a green liquid but now it was capsules so I decided that I would try holding it in my mouth until I could spit it out. It worked thank God. I didn't see the Dr. for several days. It was obvious that he wasn't going to be of any help and he didn't really have any interest in me or my problem. Also I'm sure he knew all about the orderlies use of Thorazine. Everyone did. If he hadn't wanted them to give it to me he would have told them not to. I only needed to make it for 30 days and I would be sent back to the Prison. I was already looking forward to that.

One day they told me that they needed someone who was mentally competent to work in the kitchen and I volunteered. The eating area was screened in with chain link fencing and had a sliding gate also covered with chain link. I helped serve the food and after the meals washed trays and silverware and counted all of the silverware. No knives, just spoons and forks. One day there was a fork missing. I counted again. Yes it was missing. They got ready to search every one and one of the inmates, a young man, about my age, reached into his pocket pulled out the fork and threw it at me. I was sure I hadn't made any friends. This particular person had been committed by a court because he had killed someone and had been found not guilty by reason of insanity. You could tell that he had once had a body builders physique and you could tell just by looking at his eyes that really was nuts and he was dangerous. They didn't do anything to him. No point in it. But he kept looking at me. I'd glance at him every now and then and he was staring at me.

The bathrooms were a long tiled room probably 30 foot by 10 foot with sinks to the left and stalls to the right and open showers at the far end. The water in the sinks was so hot you could make really hot instant coffee with it right out of the tap. We smoked cigarettes on the ward and we had 1 gallon cans with water in them that we used for ash trays and we would empty them in the toilet. We were watching TV that evening and he seemed to have forgotten about me so I got up to make myself a cup of coffee. We had large tin cups and I put a spoon of instant coffee in it and went in the bathroom to get water. As I turned from the sink to walk out I met him coming in with a butt can in his hand held by the rim. As we passed I saw the hate in his eyes and I guessed what he was going to do and I wasn't wrong. I glanced over my right shoulder as he walked by and saw him spin around with the can raised to bring it down on my head but he didn't get the chance to finish his move. I spun around to my right with that very hot cup of coffee in my right hand and threw it in his face, came up with my left hand and grabbed him by the throat and took him down to the floor. I don't think I hit him I can't remember for sure but his head bounced off that tile floor pretty hard. The can and the cup bouncing around on that tile floor made quite a racket so the orderlies were in there pretty quick. They were bound and determined they were going to tranquilize me with thorazine or something else but I finally convinced them not to. Instead they locked me in a cell for the night. That was alright. I felt safe in there. They naturally reported the incident to the Dr. and he came to see me the next day and I told him I wanted to go back to the prison so he sent me back. I could survive in the prison but I wasn't sure about the state hospital.

I was glad to get out of there and back to my cell. I felt way safer there. I didn't feel good though, just kind of tired and spaced out. I thought it might be the heavy medication they had me on so I got some books from the library about epilepsy and the various drugs they use for it and the side effects. One thing I read was that If you are in fact not an epileptic and you take these drugs they can actually cause you to have seizures. I remembered what that old country doctor had said when I had the first seizure. He said it was not epilepsy, so I decided to try something. They gave me medications at the prison but never really paid attention whether or not I took them so I started cutting down on them. By the time I was paroled I wasn't taking so much as an aspirin, and I wasn't having seizures. My mind was way sharper too. They thought it was because of the new medication I was on.

The day before I was released they had me see a Dr. at the prison. It was a woman Dr. who I had never seen before. She must have come over from the state hospital. She wrote a prescription for those medications I was supposed to be taking and gave it to me. She told me that I would have to take them for the rest of my life and if I ever stopped taking them I would go into a grand mal seizure and I would die. I never filled that prescription.

Chapter Six: Prison Riot

◇◇◇◇

One day while at school in French class, we could hear yelling and alarm bells. Smelled smoke and heard things crashing so we checked it out and discovered that we were in the middle of a full blown riot. We had some decisions to make and quick. When this started the guards that were in the school ran for the control center. Some were captured and taken to the yard. But at any rate that meant the school was unprotected and we had a young pretty French teacher in there that was trapped with a bunch of male convicts. We knew it wouldn't take long before the rioters would be coming up the stairs. They had already set things on fire down below and smoke was coming up the stairs and through the air vents. We had a meeting and decided we would take bookbinding tape, about what we now call Duct tape, *(Duct tape as it is now called didn't exist then.)* and tape all of the doors shut to keep the rioters out and all the vents shut to keep the smoke out. And we said we would protect the teacher with our lives if necessary. There were about a dozen of us up there that day and we all liked and respected her. We also decided that anyone who wanted to leave before it was all taped up could. I decided that I would leave so I went down the stairs and observed that the prison store, which was just a little alcove near the foot of the stairs, had been taken over and cleaned out of cigarettes and snacks The mess hall was being commandeered for anything that could be used on the yard for the long haul. Looking back on it at this point in time I guess what has been going on in Wisconsin with the Unions is a pretty fair comparison except Wisconsin I believe is actually worse. There was a furniture factory in an industrial building on the way out to the exercise yard where the convicts were taught wood working skills and beautiful desks were made. I had been told that the Governors desk had even been made there. Smoke was coming out of the broken windows on the front of the building. Smoke was also pouring out of the cell blocks where mattresses had been set on fire. The National Guard and State Police were on the wall with M 16s and shot guns. A prison guard who was a lieutenant and had made it a point to dress and act like a lieutenant in Hitler's SS had been captured and was being marched blind folded with his hands tied out to the yard.

A friend who I had known in Vale and arrived at the prison chained to, a young man from Kansas, was about to join in the mayhem when I found him and got him aside and explained to him that the very smartest thing we could do was stick together, watch each other's back and stay alive till this was over. And above all else, don't commit any prosecutable crimes, as this would probably be on tape. Thank God he listened to me.

Someone else had broken into the furniture factory and set it on fire so we walked in through an open door to see if we could find anything inside to arm ourselves with. There was a box of wrenches. About 16 inches long and as I recall they were inch and one eighth. I have no Idea what they were for but they made a formidable and visible deterrent stuck in our belts. We looked around and found four of our buddies who we normally hung around with and we all stuck together and stayed out of trouble till it was over. Nobody messed with us.

There was no food on the yard other than candy bars and chips that came from the store when it was broken into. We did have coffee though. Someone had brought a two gallon can of ground coffee from the mess hall. A fire was built with broken boards from the bleachers and a big stainless pot full of water was placed on the fire and a clean cotton sock full of coffee was boiled to make coffee. It wasn't great but I've had worse. (I think, though I can't quite remember when.)

Things went pretty well and nobody got killed. Though a few people did get a few bruises. There was a weight lifting area that was covered with a roof where the guards were held where they couldn't be observed from the guard towers. , some of the guards got roughed up a little. I think probably because they couldn't understand that for the moment at least they weren't in charge and they got mouthy. There was a group of convicts, mostly lifers that had planned the riot. It wasn't just a spur of the moment thing, although most of us didn't know about it in advance. I know that I didn't. There were actually people in charge and some of the lifers that were, negotiated the terms for ending the riot without loss of life but with conditions. The warden got fired. Most of the conditions were eventually met. And oh yes, they took the teacher and the convicts out of the top floor of the school while the riot was still in progress with a hook and ladder truck from outside the wall. They had to send someone up with a cutting torch first to cut the bars off the window to get them out. And yes the teacher was fine. She sent a letter of thanks to her class for protecting her but school was out and she never came back.

They locked us down for about a week while things got put back into a semblance of order. Some of the men who beat up guards were taken back to court and given more time and sent to another prison. We got a new visitors center where we could actually sit down with our family, kiss wives and girl friends, hold children in laps, etc. I didn't have a wife anymore. She had divorced me and remarried. Some friends came to visit though, that I had been best man for at their wedding several years before in happier times and his wife planted a big wet kiss on me. That was nice. I'd forgotten how nice a kiss could be. We got a new mess hall and some of our resident artists painted a mural on the wall and we had individual tables for four. You could sit where you wished with who you wished to sit with, and you could talk. No more guards patrolling with shotguns. They painted the cells pastel colors, *before they had been an ugly green,* and the bars were repainted blue instead of the traditional battle ship grey. We had a committee who would present grievances to the warden. This was all important stuff and it made a difference, especially if you have to spend the rest of your life in there. It was still the joint though and it was still a bad place to be. Some things never change.

Chapter Seven: Still Doing' Time.

❖❖❖❖

Everything inside the wall was burned or smoke damaged so no more school for a while. I wanted out of my cell so I applied for and got a job in the laundry. I became of all things a shirt presser. I was really quite good at it. I got along well with everyone there almost. The pads and the covers for the machines were kept upstairs in kind of a loft and there was none there because one of the guys had stashed them for his own use. I went up and looked to make sure there were none up there and then told him that I needed one that he had stashed. First he refused and I got a little hot and he said he would take me up and show me where they were. He went in the office and got a pair of scissors about a foot long and started for the stairs. I said just a minute and I went and got another pair of scissors and headed after him. He suddenly decided he would give me a pad and cover after all. That was something else I learned in there. If something looks dangerous it probably is and hope for the best but prepare for the worst.

The cells had two bunks in them one above the other, hinged to the wall and suspended from chains, but most of the time I was by myself. I had one cell partner who I had actually met in California. It seems like once some of these people get in the system they never learn and just keep coming back, even from joint to joint. Actually I think they get used to being taken care of in an institutional environment until they are not able to take care of themselves. I had been thinking about getting a cell partner just for company. We talked on the yard and seemed to get along all right and we thought it might be less boring so we decided to try it. After about a week he wanted out as I went to bed one night while he was writing a letter and I started snoring. He woke me and said that I was snoring. That night I found out that sleep deprivation is a very powerful thing. After about the 5th time of being woke up and told I was snoring I found myself holding him up against the wall with his throat in my hand and I didn't even remember getting there. The next day he was gone.

A short time later he made parole and was gone about a month and was violated. He got picked up with a gun in his glove compartment. So he not only had to finish his sentence but he had a new charge as well and consequently more time. Then about 6 months later my young friend from Kansas moved in. We got along good. I tried to be a good influence on him and keep him out of trouble as he seemed to have a penchant for making mistakes in judgement. That's why he was there. I guess because my folks were from Kansas I felt like I was his big brother.

Then who should show up again but Denny. He had finally gotten caught for some of his mischief but as soon as he saw me, he started telling me about the scheme's he had for when he got out. He and his wife were still together living in Portland and I think he only had a 3 year sentence but he couldn't wait till we got out and we could score. I told him I was not interested but he could still dream. I was up for parole a short time after that and was denied because I didn't have a job to go to. Shortly after that I was approved to work outside the walls and they let me work in the prison auto body shop as I had had some experience and some training. I think I was out there about 3 months and I went back to see the parole board and this time they approved it "If I could find a job." There was a minister that had been my mother's minister who was living in Salem that heard about my plight from my mother and he arranged to pick me up from the prison and take me job hunting. It was a shock to my system to be out in the real world and not have handcuffs or shackles on. One place I went to fill out an application I walked down a long ramp down on the waterfront and around a corner and up a flight of stairs and I was all by myself and it was scary. I had been under someone else's control for so long it was frightening to actually be in charge of myself, if only for a few minutes. We went out to lunch and set at a lunch counter and when I wanted more coffee I held my cup in the air. Well, that's the way I've done it for the last five years. He whispered to me that I shouldn't do that on the outside. It was very embarrassing. I got a job as the body man for Earl Scheib, home of the $19.95 paint job, on 82nd street in Portland. I could stay in a half way house. Everything was coming together. I was really going to be free again.

One night, before I actually got out I had a dream that I think I'll remember for the rest of my days. I dreamed I got out of prison and ran into a guy on the outside that I had been in prison with. In my dream he had a gun and car jacked a truck while I was with him and shot and killed the driver. Then he did it again and killed someone else then he did it again. The next thing I remember in my dream was I had gotten away from him and gone back to the prison and I had broken into the prison and was hiding in a cell. I woke up in a cold sweat. I never associated with anyone who I had been in prison with when I got out. I thought of that dream often.

I was scheduled to be released at 8:00 am and my folks were sitting in the waiting room of the prison waiting to pick me up. I was sitting in the holding area inside the prison in the corner of the control center waiting to be released. Ever so often one of the cons walking through would stop and tell me not to worry about getting out. "You'll be back" they would say. I swore I wouldn't. The reason I hadn't been released on time was that someone who had my release papers had not came to work that morning. Imagine that. Patience is a virtue saith the Lord. About 2 pm I finally was released. Dad drove me into Portland and I really had to talk to keep from being fired before I got started as they were expecting me that morning. Dad took me to Sears where I bought some tools, took the tools to the shop and then took me to the half way house, said goodbye and I got settled in.

Chapter Eight: A New Beginning.

◇◇◇◇

The next day I took a bus to work and about 10 minutes to quitting time, a baby blue Buick pulled up in the parking lot. It was Denny's wife Kay. I guess I must have told Denny where I would be working and he told Kay. Kay was about 26 years old I think. She was a very attractive and intelligent girl. I'd met her before when I'd gone to their house in Portland with my wife in 63. And I'd been in the visiting room when she had come in to see Denny about 4 months ago.

I really did like Kay. She was cute and sexy and she knew it. From the clothes she wore, the way her hair and nails were obviously professionally done, even to the car she was driving she just radiated class. Someone who didn't know her would never have guessed that she was a high class call girl and that she was married to a petty thief. She made a lot more money than she could make any other way for her and her kids and she looked and acted like a lady, most of the time. I think Denny was largely responsible for the prostitution at least when she first started. At that time she couldn't have been more than 17. She didn't sleep with just anyone or stand on a corner and pick men up. She had repeat clients. And they paid her well. All she really wanted to be though was a good mother. She was really good with her children, two boys and a girl and they were kept completely away from all of this. Men were never brought to her house. However I didn't think I should be seen with her and I didn't know if my parole officer was watching me or not. It would take a lot longer than this to get comfortable with my new freedom. I talked to her about it and said I would see my parole officer the next day and I would get back to her. She gave me her phone number and I took a bus home.

The next day I saw my parole officer and he set it up to see him about once a month, more or less. He seemed very nice but I was afraid he might be giving me enough rope to hang myself so I made a mental note to be good and be careful. I also told him about Kay. Told him who she was and who her husband was and pretty much the whole story. Turned out Denny had a long record but Kay had never been arrested . He said he had no problem with me associating with her if I wanted to but when Denny got out to stay away from him. So I called Kay that afternoon and we went out to dinner that night. She had a friend who ran a service station who had a 60 Olds that I could buy from him for no money down and 50 dollars a month. I called my parole officer and he said fine but to get insurance on it. I also had to get my driving license. I had been in prison long enough that I no longer had a suspended license on my record so I could legally get my license back. I got a book and studied it for a few minutes and passed my written test and the next day they let me off work for an hour and I passed the driving test.

Everything went pretty smooth for a while and I moved out of the halfway house and into a shared houseboat on the

Columbia river across from Jantzen Beach. Kay and I had became pretty good friends and I enjoyed being around her and the kids and a family environment. I really craved that after the years I had spent in prison. After a few months though, I realized that I had to get away from Kay as she thought she was falling in love with me and I liked her more than I should and I knew that would mean trouble when Denny got out. We talked about it and she knew I was right. I said goodbye that night and I never saw her or Denny again. I've often wondered how her life turned out.

The Owner of the house boat, Bob and an Oro wheat truck driver, Jim, and I lived on it. It had 3 bedrooms and a full bath, a laundry room and a boat dock downstairs with a yellow 16 foot Sea Ray ski boat parked at the dock. Upstairs it had a kitchen and a bar at least 20 feet long, and a 100 gallon fish tank with one large Piranha in it. There was another tank in the upstairs bathroom built in under the counter top that had Guppy's in it to feed to the Piranha. I never understood why but the girls seemed to get a thrill from dropping a Guppy into the tank and watching the Guppy get eaten by the Piranha. The last thing the Piranha would eat was the head, and the head was still trying to swim. I came to the conclusion that I would probably never understand women.

There was a big deck outside above the dock that the boat was tied to. One thing about that arrangement was if the girls wanted to go for a boat ride at midnight they had to go through the bedroom to get to the boat. It was Bob's boat and Bob's bedroom. He had it all figured out. We had a lot of party's on the house boat, usually on Friday night. Bob was the president of a local singles club. His little black book was a 4 drawer filing cabinet in his bedroom. I think most of the single girls phone numbers and vital statistics in the city's of Portland, Vancouver, and outlying areas were in that cabinet.

It was a very fun situation to find myself in after the years I'd spent behind bars. No one knew anything about my history. I didn't lie to anyone. They didn't ask and I didn't tell. My parole officer came out one day after I'd got moved in when no one else was home and I told him I didn't intend to tell anyone anything about myself. He said that was my business and that if he wanted to see me he would let me know. He wanted me to make it. Contrary to what I had heard, from the cons on the inside, the parole officers are on your side if they see that you are really trying to make it.

Believe it or not though, all of the partying was starting to be a little boring. A lot of the people I found myself partying with were empty suits and empty heads. The girl's came to our party's because they were lonely and thrill seekers. The guys who came were mostly predators. Actually some of the girls were too. Kay had way more class than any of them did. They just weren't my kind of people. Besides, if I was going to make it I needed to get serious and prove to myself just how responsible I could be.

Sometimes I would be out of food and hungry by payday. Actually I'm sure I could have done better but I needed to get my priorities in order. Meantime a 20 cent box of macaroni and cheese and a loaf of bread would last me for a couple of days. A quart of milk for a quarter and I was in hog heaven. Needless to say I wasn't gaining weight. The manager of the body shop would stop selling body work when I got close to making my quota when I was supposed to get 50% commission for the remainder of the week. So I was only making 2.25 an hour which was about par back then but still not great.

Minimum wage was $1.25, Gas was .25 a gallon, rent was 40.00 a month, cigarettes were 2.00 a carton. You could get a decent hamburger for a quarter. Levies were 3.50. Yeah you could get by but I was ready for a change so I discussed it with my parole officer and quit my job and headed for Glendale, my old home town. A few days later I was pulling green chain at the local lumber mill. Although I'd gotten used to the big city, I was still a country boy at heart. I know that very little happens in a small town that everyone doesn't know about so they all must have known where I had been, but no one ever mentioned it, even the local deputy. We even got to be pretty good friends. I was making about the same money pulling green chain as I'd been making doing body work plus I was getting some overtime when I wanted it working at the plywood or at the green veneer mill. So a couple of double shifts a week at around 5.00 an hour and things were looking up. Once in awhile I would go to Portland to visit but I was quite happy being home again. I was living at my folks place which was good for me financially but dad got fed up with it as I still had a little partying to get out of my system and I'm sure he thought I was going to get into trouble again. Anyway it was easier on everyone involved if I didn't live there, so I moved out and got my own place. I was told later by dad that it used to be a chicken house but I didn't believe it as it had knotty pine paneling on the walls and ceiling and it was still way better than a cell. It didn't take much to please me those days.

Chapter Nine:
Cars Pickups and Carpenters

◆◆◆◆

It seemed that I was a little harder to please when it came to my cars though. That Olds had been a really great car but one night coming home from work in a rainstorm in Portland a bottom radiator hose let go. The first I knew I had a problem was when I pushed down on the gas and it started spark knocking. The engine was nearly froze up. Once I got the hose and the wiring replaced that was melted and with the help of a 24 volt booster it finally started and ran but it was never the same after that. I'm sure it took the tension out of the rings and did damage to the lifters. It still started and ran pretty good though the lifters rattled when it was cold so I let one of my girlfriends have it and I found a 63 Plymouth with a solid lifter 318 in it. It ran like it had a hot cam in it. I think it may have been a cop car before I got it because it sure was fast. Then one day while driving around Portland I saw the front end of a car sticking out of a ramshackle garage. The next day I stopped and knocked on the door. A young man answered the door and I asked him if he wanted to sell it and could I look at it. It turned out it was a 1960 Dodge Phoenix convertible. It was obvious it had been used for drag racing as it had an expensive Sun tach, ladder bars and some other race things. The motor was a 360 and didn't run and the transmission had been rebuilt by AMCO but it was toast also. The top was in tatters and it didn't even have wheels on it. However the body was straight and the interior was good, the seats and door panels and all the glass was good, and it had a beautiful boot cover that was black tuck and roll. It was love at first sight. I gave him $25.00 for it, bought some junk yard wheels and tires and towed it home. I found a 1960 Chrysler Saratoga in the paper that had been wrecked and had all the parts I needed. I think I paid fifty dollars for that. I used a shade tree limb at a girlfriends brothers house to pull the motor. I bought a new top from sears and installed it myself. I bought some chrome rims and tires from Big O tires and in a couple of months I had it on the road. I think I enjoyed that car more than any vehicle I ever had. Maybe it was because I built it myself. When I came to Glendale I had sold the 63 Plymouth to the girlfriend who had let me use her brothers shade tree limb and the Phoenix was all I had.

This was a particularly interesting trip that I think I should include. It just goes to prove that life can be dangerous no matter how hard you try to keep your nose clean.

I was just coming out of Portland on I-5, heading south near Wilsonville when I stopped at a truck stop service station to fill up. It was a cool evening so I had my top up. I went to the bathroom while the young man filled the tank and washed my windshield. I went in and paid the bill and when I came out there was a very rough looking guy standing by the drivers door of my car. I asked him what his problem was and he said that he didn't have one but I did. He said to get in the car and something about him looked familiar and my spider sense was tingling so I did as he said. When I got in I saw that three others were in the back seat already, one man and two girls. He went around the car and got in and he told me to start the engine and head south. I did as he said then he started talking. He said he and a buddy, the one in the back seat, had just gotten out of Walla Walla state pen in Washington and they were headed for Ashland Oregon and that they were Hells Angels out of Oakland California and that I was going to take them there. I had just been car jacked.

First he said his name was "Chains," then he told me he was Sonny Barger, The pres. of the Oakland chapter of the Angels. I had met Sonny down in Oakland about 8 years before when I was working for Western Union and I really didn't know if he was telling the truth or not. He had been clean shaven but with long hair when I'd known him before and this guy had a lot of hair on his face so along with the added years and 40 miles of bad road it was hard to tell for sure but I didn't dispute his word. I knew he was a Hells Angel because he was wearing his Colors, I just wasn't sure he was Sonny. I told him I'd been in Oakland when I was working for western union and that I'd hung out where they had hung out and I'd met him down there. We got to talking about it and he said like, oh yeah, I remember you too. I don't think he really did but we had a good trip that took about 3 hours and I went ahead and took them to one of their buddies place in Ashland, we said goodbye and good luck and then I went back to Glendale. If I'd been some smart mouthed college preppie that could have turned out a lot different. The only problem I had from that encounter was that they were smoking pot while we were traveling and the smell got into the material of the top and I had to put my top down for the rest of the summer and I think this was only April. I sure didn't want a cop or a parole officer to stick their nose in there

The Robert Dollar Co. 1970

The boss at the sawmill thought he could make better use of me than pulling green chain so he started trying me out and training me at various jobs in the mill. First it was spotting for the trim saw. Good thing I was young and strong as that was a young man's job. I lost weight and was in better shape than I'd ever been in my life, even when I had been lifting weights. Wow. Then He taught me to run the resaw. That was a work house too. Then grading for the resaw. Then One day he asked me if I'd like to learn to tail saw. I said I didn't know what that was so he said "come on, I'll show you". He took me down to the head saw. That's the saw that breaks the logs down when they first come in the mill. He told me to watch the man pulling the slabs off behind the saw, and he left. This guy had a tank top on, great big arms, and more hair on his back then a Shetland pony. If I'd seen him in the woods I would have thought he was a Sasquatch. I watched him all night and that night after work the boss asked me if I thought I could do it and before I could say anything he said "You better be able to cause you're the new tail sawyer starting Monday night."(this was Friday night.) I did that Job off and on for the next three years.

I got a phone call from a girlfriend in Portland about this time. She said the brakes had went out on the Olds that I'd given to her and she had ran into the back of a truck. No one was hurt but it had totaled the Olds and she needed a car and could I help. I kind of felt responsible since it was my car and I'd had trouble with the brakes before. She was on welfare and had four kids and she didn't have anyone else to turn to for this kind of help. I went to Portland that weekend and she had found a 67, Plymouth Belvedere coupe for very little money, trouble being it had a slant six engine and a Valiant floor shift 3 speed transmission that someone had put in it that wouldn't shift gears. I took it to check it out and discovered it had no grease in the transmission. I gave the owner of it 50 dollars for it, on the educated guess that was what was wrong with it. I took it home and filled the transmission with 90 weight oil and it shifted fine after that. She was happy and I junked what was left of the Olds and went back to Glendale.

A few weeks later I saw an ad in the paper for a 1960 Chevy station wagon for $10.00. They said the brakes were out. I knew how to rebuild brakes so I went to see it. It had a good 6 cylinder engine and an automatic transmission that seemed to be perfect. The interior was near perfect and after a wash and wax job the paint (red and white) was even good. I bought it and took it home and rebuilt the brakes. It needed besides shoes, a master cylinder and 2 wheel cylinders. The girl friend in Portland had said she would rather have a station wagon any way for her kids, so this would be great. I did a tune up on it too then I took it to Portland and swapped her and brought the Plymouth home. I cleaned the Plymouth up and fixed a few things on it and started driving it around town with a for sale sign on it. It wasn't long till I was approached by a young man who was the owner of a 1968 Olds 442 that he had swerved to miss a deer with and had side swiped a tree instead and ran over a big rock as well. He wanted to trade me for the Plymouth as he needed a car to drive. I didn't really need the Plymouth and I was intrigued by the Olds and I thought I could fix it so I made the deal and brought the Olds home. The rock that he had ran over had made a big dent in the pan and the crank was hitting it and making a terrible racket. I had to lift the engine about a foot to get the pan off but with the help of my little brother who I think was about 12 then and a rafter in my dads garage we got it done , then with a block of wood and a sledge hammer got the pan straightened out and back on the car. That engine purred like a little kitty cat. Over a period of about 6 months I replaced the quarter panel, the door and the front fender and the windshield.

The mill used to shut down at midnight so you had time to have a drink after work so one night I went down town after work and I met a young man who I'll call Dave Freestone. He was, he said a carpenter, and he had a chance to build some houses over at Central Point but he needed a partner. I'd always wanted to learn how to build houses. He said I could make $5.00 an hour. That was twice what I was making. It was working in the day time instead of at night. That would be nice. So to check to see if he was telling me the truth about the job, he and I went to Central Point and talked to the General Contractor who confirmed that we had a job but Dave was a sub-contractor and I would be working for Dave so how much I made was up to Dave and How fast we could build a house. I quit my Job after phoning my parole officer and started building houses. Shortly after I started building houses I discovered that I needed a pickup more than I needed a hot rod, plus, the Olds was very fast and I had almost gotten killed one day when I got into a race on the highway. The other car, a Chrysler had swerved into the left hand lane in front of me narrowly missing me and I had hit the brakes and went into a spin. I went around and around at close to 100 miles an hour. God must have other plans for me because I had absolutely no control over the situation and I really could have died that day . I traded it straight across for a nice little orange 60 Chevy pickup with a black diamond tuck interior.

When I knew I might have a problem was after we had the walls up on the first house Dave had to smoke a joint with his lunch. He was worthless the rest of the day. But we finally got it and another one built over a period of about 4 weeks. I made probably about $5.00 an hour. We then got a job with Cap Homes building a house up by Klamath Falls, way out from any place. The name of the area was Sprague River. It was high desert country about 50 miles from Klamath Falls Oregon. Building for Capp homes is different. You have a building package sitting beside a foundation. They are supposed to be pre-cut. You just put them together. We were sleeping in a tent and the people who were the owners of the house were living in a travel trailer and were feeding us. I don't think that was part of the deal they were just very nice people and we must have looked hungry and we got to be good friends. I seem to recall the lady mentioning something about me reminding her of her son and also there was no place else to eat, way out there so if they wanted a house built I guess that was how we had to do it.

We got right to work on the house and we soon had the floor finished and were ready to start putting up the walls. As I said It was all pre-cut and all you do is put it together, so it was going pretty fast. We framed the front wall and the front wall of the garage. Complete with doors, windows entryway, and black insulation board with it lying on the deck. We enlisted the help of some neighbors that afternoon to stand it up. Everything was going great and we were ahead of schedule. Well, it seemed that every day at about the same time a gust of wind would come through, blow for about a minute than quit. We had braced the wall when we stood it up with about eight 10 ft 2x4s and nailed them to the deck and to the top of the wall. The wind started to blow and it blew the wall towards the house and bowed the 2x4s like a spring and when it stopped blowing as suddenly as it had begun, the force of those 2X4s straightening out threw that whole wall out into the middle of the yard right on top of our building package, not only breaking the wall and almost everything in it but much of what it landed on as well.

There was nothing to do but take it apart and see what we could salvage, make a list of what we couldn't and call our boss and order new material from Copeland Lumber in Klamath Falls. Someone found our blue prints on top of a hill tangled up in sage brush over a mile away. It took about a week to get enough materials to finish the wall and another week to get the windows and doors that had gotten ruined when the wall went down but about two weeks after that we finally got the roof on. Dave ran out of Pot and was kind of hard to get along with for awhile but I think that made him work harder, kind of with a sense of urgency. He wanted to get finished so we could get back to civilization so he could "score some weed". I had heard that that stuff wasn't addictive but I think that's a lie. We weren't quite finished by Labor Day but we needed a break so we drove down to Grants Pass to enjoy the holiday. We stopped at the Rogue State Park as there were boat races and all kinds of festivities going on. This was in 1971 and the hippy movement was in full swing. Dave saw a VW van pull into the parking lot with flowers painted on it and he thought surely he could get something to smoke there. When the van stopped a man and several young girls got out dressed in the hippy attire that was so popular those days. The man had a long beard and looked like he belonged on a movie set for "Moses" and the girls had on long dresses decorated with beads and embroidery and flowers in their hair. Dave went to talk to him and suddenly the man stretched out his arms and in a very loud voice said: "JESUS CHRIST WOULD NOT SELL YOU DRUGS"! Naturally every one turned to look. Dave came running back to the pickup and said,: "Let's get out of here, Jesus freaks." Later that night he went somewhere by himself and found a very small amount of "stems and pieces." I had never been around these "Hippy" people before and I didn't do drugs as I really liked to be in control of myself and my mind. Dave didn't know my history and I didn't tell him so he didn't understand why I was so "strait laced." I was never interested in drugs as I had been forcibly stoned on prescription drugs for many years and I really didn't like the feeling of not being in control, and in the back of my mind I always wondered if it could make me start having seizures again. Also I knew it would be a good way to wind up back in prison as there were people in there who had been caught with pot seeds in the carpet of their car and wound up with a 5 year sentence so I didn't even want it in my car

Chapter Ten: Hippie's and TeePee's

◇◇◇◇

We drove over to Glendale so I could see my folks and we visited with my parents and had a good home cooked meal. Then Dave wanted to go to upper Cow Creek to see some people he knew and score on some higher grade weed he said so later we drove up there. I was familiar with that area as that was where my ex wife had lived when we were going together so I couldn't understand why the place he said he was taking me didn't sound familiar. I had hunted deer there also and I couldn't recall any houses being in that area. Suddenly he said "Turn here." I stopped and said "But there is no road here." And he said "Drive through the creek". So I did, and through the trees and along the creek for probably a quarter of a mile and we came out in a secluded meadow about a quarter of a mile away from the road. You would need a helicopter to find that place if you didn't know it was there. It was on BLM land. There was a cabin made of logs and rough sawn boards maybe 300 square feet and a teepee with about a 16 foot floor space. There were children playing, some with no clothes on. There was a garden with veggies and probably pot growing in it. I had no Idea what pot even looked like back then. There seemed to be about four family's living there. They were dressed a lot like the family we had encountered in the park the day before. The cabin had a fire hole in the floor lined with rocks and a sleeping loft in the back half of the cabin. In the front it was open to the rafters with the gable open and the smoke would go out the gable. I was impressed with the ingenuity of the cabin, but I was more than impressed with the teepee. One little fire in the middle of the floor in a ring of rocks, kept that teepee warm as toast and the reflection off the white walls gave plenty of light to read a paper. The outer shell of the teepee lacked a few inches of reaching the ground but an inner skirt about 3 feet high went all around the inside and the bottom of the skirt was buried in a trench in the dirt. That blocked any breeze but created a draft for the fire and you couldn't even smell smoke in there. A few rugs and blankets on the floor and what a cozy place to be. We spent the night and I was invited to stay in the teepee. It was cold that night, in the 20s, but the teepee was warm. I came away thinking that the Indians that invented these things were pretty smart. Hippy's were not too dumb. This was way better than a traditional white man's tent. I found myself wishing I had one in Sprague River. Anyway Dave got his Pot. We said goodbye and headed back to civilization and back to Sprague River to finish our job.

After we were finished in Sprague River we went back to Medford and looked up the Contractor that had hired us. He said he couldn't pay us until the place was inspected Dave borrowed my pickup that night and got picked up for drunk driving. He called me from the jail and told me where my truck was. I got there about two minutes ahead of the tow truck. Dave wound up getting 30 days in the slammer. I went over to the contractor's house after the inspection and attempted to get paid but he said he could only pay Dave that Dave would have to pay me. When Dave got out of jail he went to see the contractor, cashed the check and I have not seen him again to this day.

I thought I was a Journeyman carpenter after building a few houses though so I went looking for another job, as a carpenter. There were a few Union jobs going on so I went to the Union Hall and put my name in and sit down and waited. About an hour later a guy asked me if I wanted to help build an apartment house in Ashland. After that I went to Grants Pass and helped build another apartment building. I ran out of work there so I drove to Portland one weekend and found a job working for a remodeler, remodeling low income housing. Then I helped someone else build a house. Eventually all of the framing and remodeling jobs dried up and I went back to Glendale and went back to work in the Sawmill. They always needed help.

Chapter Eleven: Sawmills:
the Hippie House and Matrimony

❖❖❖❖

The saw mill night shift would shut down around Christmas time every year it seemed and you could take a layoff and draw unemployment or go to work in the green veneer mill or the plywood until spring and go back to work in the sawmill. I went to work in the veneer mill as that was part of the rules of my parole was that I stayed employed. I also got all of the overtime I could handle so the money was good. I had about made up my mind at this time that I was going to stop running around the country and trying different things. I had about had all of the adventures that I could handle. Dad was still working over on the coast and mother needed help more and more. After all that I had put them through I owed them big time. I started to feel like I was needed by my family and also I think I was finally starting to grow up a little. The little town of Glendale was starting to feel like an old friend to me. Glendale Oregon was a rompin' stompin' lumber town back in those days. There were a couple of bars in town and there was live music and dancing in at least one of them every weekend. One evening I met a girl down there that was a cousin to a friend of mine and I wound up taking her out. The next weekend I ran into her again at the bar and she introduced me to a friend of hers. As it worked out her friend and I started dating . Meanwhile my mother needed to have surgery and my father asked me if any of my girlfriends had nursing experience. " Actually yes" I said." I have this friend and her name is Nancy, and she has told me that she has worked as a certified nursing assistant before she came to Glendale." So Nancy moved into my parent's house to take care of my mother when she came home from the hospital. One day when we were over at Medford I asked her to marry me. She asked me if I knew what I was saying. Meanwhile I turned and looked over my shoulder as I thought someone else had spoken the words that came out of my mouth. A few weeks later we were married by a judge at the courthouse in Grants Pass Oregon with my mother as a witness and my little brother as best man.

We hadn't actually meant to get married that day, at least I hadn't. It was a week day and I had to work that night but for some reason I had brought my mother and my little brother along. I thought we were only going to get a license to get married. We had planned on getting married at my parents home in Glendale but we hadn't thought about Grants Pass being Josephine Co. and Glendale being in Douglas County. We could either go to Roseburg for the license or get married then and there or forget the whole thing. So as it turned out, we had to hurry and find a judge, get it done and hurry home 'cause I had to get my lunch, change my clothes and get to work. Nancy had to hurry home too cause she would have to baby sit my (our now) white German Sheppard. (How romantic.) I got off work at midnight though so it all worked out.

We lived in quite a collection of diverse places in the almost 40 years we have been married, as we moved around a lot. Some places were pretty nice and some not so nice but I think we had more fun and have more memories of that shack at the confluence of cow creek and rattlesnake creek than anyplace else that we've been. The place was hardly livable when I moved in there but at the time I was a bachelor and I thought it was fine. I picked up a bed at an auction I believe, bought a wood heater at the local building supply store, had to put in a chimney 'cause the last people had just put a stove pipe through the wall and almost burned it down. I bought a second hand (or maybe third hand) electric drop in range and had someone build a plywood cabinet for it. An X girlfriend had sold me a refrigerator that she had in her tack room in her barn. I had a radio and a tape player. Eight tracks were the thing then. I also had an eight track player in my pickup. I was in Heaven. Then it rained and the roof leaked. We were married then. It had a flat roof,(Or nearly so) so I got some lumber from work and framed up a roof right over the other roof, I got some reject plywood from the company plywood mill for just about free, then I decided to really save some money and just buy some rolled roofing instead of shingles as it would be quicker and easier to put on or so I thought. I had never installed rolled roofing before and I thought I should hide my nails like when you are roofing with shingles so I only nailed the top and lapped the bottom. We had a rainstorm with wind right after that and it blew my rolled roofing off and right out into the yard. The next time I put it on it got nailed everywhere. I was out by that old place about 5 years ago. The house was still there and the roof was still on. That's 30 years and counting. I bought a picture window from somewhere and installed it in the side of the house so she could look out the window at her flowers. That was a wedding present.

The property that the old shack sat on was 40 acres with two creek frontages. I paid $40.00 a month rent and I was supposed to look after the fences and keep the place up, Kind of. Actually he said I could do anything I wanted to including burn the house down just don't bother him with it. We got our water from a gravity feed system from a spring that had supplied water for 3 houses for a number of years. The first year we lived there the spring went dry. I tried digging out the spring but it seemed to have expired, so I put a pump in Rattlesnake creek and laid plastic pipe to the house. The water tasted good and made good coffee. I never had it tested and we never got sick so I guess it was ok. That spring was actually pretty nasty with waterdogs and frogs and God knows what crawling around in it. I think the creek was probably better. It had rainbow trout and crawdads in it.

We decided since we had all that property at our disposal we should do something with it so we bought some wiener pigs from the foreman over at the mill. Then we got some Cornish Cross baby chicks that we went in on partners with friends on. The chickens grew into friars in no time at all and our friends came out and we spent an entire day butchering chickens. I never wanted to look at another chicken for awhile after that. Nancy grew up on a farm and I did too in the early years of my childhood, so we were both quite literally in hog heaven. Between pigs and chickens, silver grey Squirrels, dogs and cats, porcupines, skunks, deer and rattlesnakes, we had quite a farm. We actually tried to eat a porcupine once. That was awful. It tasted more like the pine than the pork. We also ate a rattle snake that I had killed. That was good. Then we decided to hunt silver grey squirrels and eat them. Now that was really good and it was amazing how much meat was on those rascals. All of that came to a screeching halt however when Nancy on her way home from town one day ran over one. She saw it flopping around in the road in her rear view mirror and naturally thought she would just pick it up and take it home and put it in the freezer with the rest of them. Well by the time she got home it had come back to life and was making chirping sounds but it seemed to be paralyzed so, being the good little nurse and momma that she is she decided to nurse it back to health. When I got home she had me build a cage for it and set it next to the wood heater. She gave it range of motion therapy and it responded to it. She fed it oat meal gruel with a turkey baster. It was very cute and she named it Twinkle toes. When it got well she opened the cage in the house to let it loose. The dog got after it and they went through the house like a cyclone but it finally went out the open door and up a tree. Every squirrel we saw after that was thought to be either Twinkle Toes or one of Twinkle Toes relatives. Needless to say we never ate any more Squirrels.

Kids, Motorcycles,and dune buggies.

Nancy was born and raised in Sequim Washington and we had made a trip there before we got married as she wanted me to meet her folks her brother John and her children. She had five children, four girls and a boy. Her ex-husband had custody though and she really missed her kids. The oldest girl Lynnea was 16 I believe. The next one Debbie was 14 then the boy Duane was 13 then another girl Janet who was 12 and the youngest girl Cheryl was

11. The boy spent most of his time living and working with his Uncle John on his dairy. Her X was remarried and the girls lived with them. After we got married she really wanted to bring the two youngest girls to live with us but her X said no. Those girls missed their Momma though and had other ideas and they gave him such a hard time of it that he finally brought them down and dumped them on our door step. Then the next older girl Debbie showed up too and we had a family. I believe I was happier then than at any other time in my life.

We had bought a motorcycle before the kids came to live with us. It was almost new and we had bought it from a friend who I worked with. He was a hill climber and had bought it to use for such since it was so powerful. He had modified it with extensions to move the back wheel farther back to keep the front wheel down when climbing a steep hill It came over backwards on him anyway on a hill that they called "Whales head" down by Brookings Oregon. After that he decided it wasn't as good a hill climber bike as he thought it would be so he sold it to me. We took the extensions off and shortened the chain back up and all that remained was a dent in the gas tank and both the tachometer and the speedometer were broken off. I rode it with Nancy on behind for some time before I found a speedometer and tachometer at the bike shop to replace it with. When we found out how fast we had been riding it about scared us to death. It was a 1973 750cc Kawasaki. It was a beautiful metal flake green and it was very fast. It was a big road bike and we put a lot of miles on it in the summer time. We never wrecked it but she was always afraid of it especially after she knew how fast we were going, so we sold it about halfway through the first winter it sat on the porch. One reason that I got rid of it was the kids showed zero interest in it. Janet however would ride with me but Cheryl never would. They showed zero interest in the dune buggy too. I always wondered though why the dune buggy always had a dead battery when I wanted to start it. I found out later, much later, that when I went to work they would take the dune buggy out and play with it. The generator was 6 volt and the battery that I had was 12 volt so it wouldn't keep the battery charged, when you ran the starter. So, every time I took it out I would put it on the charger when I got back. It would have been fun to make it a family affair but for whatever reason, they were afraid of me I guess. I'm glad they had fun anyway. The friend who we had raised chickens with lived in town and had a couple of 60 cc Yamaha cycles for his two boys but he left them at our house 'cause they couldn't ride them in town. We had a big circle driveway that made a good race track so the girls got to play with them too. One day Cheryl was riding around and around and decided she needed to go to the bathroom. To solve the problem of stopping and standing it up she just ran it into the lilac bush, jumped off and ran in the house. Brilliant

One problem with paradise though was too many mouths to feed on the same income that we had just been feeding ourselves on before. Nancy was working too but it still didn't seem to be enough. I decided I had better find a way to earn more money than I was making as just a laborer in the mill. I found that the Head Saw Filer made at least double what I was making and decided to investigate that further. I asked the sawmill foreman how you got that kind of a job and he said I would have to talk to the head saw filer and ask him if he would train me. This would be the beginning of a career that would take me through the next 30 years of satisfying and nearly constant employment.

The head filer agreed to train me but it would be on his terms not mine or even the company's and especially not the Union's. I would go in on my own time and not get paid for it 3 or 4 days a week for however long it took and then I would work my regular shift on swing shift. I learned a lot from that old man that served me well from then on. Someone else was in training also that I wasn't aware of in the lower filing room and a job in that dept came up for bid after I had been in training for about 6 months.

I told Bill (the head filer) that I was going to bid on that job as I had more seniority than the other person. Bill told me that I was not going to bid on anything unless he told me I could. That was when I found out who I was really working for. It wasn't long after that though, probably a few months that Bill called me up one day and told me I would be working night shift in the filing room starting Monday. There wasn't any bidding to it. I would go to work in the filing room when Bill said I would go to work in the filing room. There was another person who worked in the mill who wanted the job though who had not been in training but had more seniority who filed a grievance but it didn't go anywhere. One night when I came in the foreman told me he wanted me to help the millwrights that night instead of working in the filing room. The next night when I got to work Bill was waiting for me and wanted to know why I hadn't done my work the night before. When I told him what had happened his face got red and he told me he would be back and he left the filing room. He came back about a half hour later and told me that I wouldn't be bothered again by that "Damn cleanup man." (The foreman had been a cleanup man before the company had made him the foreman.) I guess the poor guy had almost got fired simply because he didn't understand protocol when it came to the filing dept. Throughout my career, I had to remind people of this from time to time, sometimes the same people more than once and usually people in middle management positions.

I Am Responsible.

Things went well for awhile after that. As is life, we had good days and some days not so good, then one day I came home and there was a Oregon State vehicle in my drive. My parole officer had come for a visit. A lot of thoughts went through my head in a millisecond while I was trying to think if I had done anything wrong to prompt this visit as it was something out of the ordinary. As it was I needn't have worried. He was there with the best news that I had heard since I had been informed that my parole had been approved. He informed me that my sentence had been commuted by the Governor , 5 years early. He said he didn't think I needed any more supervision. My mind raced back to what I had learned in AA that night years ago and I knew that I wouldn't have gotten to this point without it. Thank you Lord.

As the company had a habit of doing, the sawmill shut down that fall and that time there were no options except unemployment. That was I believe 40 dollars a week. We swallowed our pride and went to Roseburg to apply for food stamps. They told me they would give me $160.00 worth of food stamps If I would give them $86.00. I told them that if I had 86.00 I wouldn't need food stamps. About that time a hippie that had been sleeping on top of a heat register all morning woke up and started cussing the guy for making him wait for so long and he gave him $300 dollars worth of food stamps for free. We went home and the next day I started going from door to door asking for work and in about two hours I had found three jobs in town building things. I had a friend who was also a family man who I worked with who was also out of work who I asked to help me and we worked together the rest of the layoff and made more money than we would have at the mill for the same period of time.

Chapter Twelve:
Sequim and Another Education

◆◆◆◆

The next phase of our life took us to Sequim Washington and my dear wife's home town and Alma Mater. We talked about it and decided maybe we could make more money and It was such a nice place to live and I could go fishing a lot and she could be close to her parents and it didn't rain, snow, blow, freeze, sleet, or hail in Sequim Washington. *at least that was what she said.* And I could go back to work building houses. So,I sublet my house just in case I wanted to come back and we packed up the kids and dogs and everything we could stick in the biggest U-Haul truck they made and we were off to Sequim. Inside we had all of our worldly belongings and the Volkswagon based dune buggy and on behind on a stiff hitch was our 1967 Thunderbird that had mysteriously lost all semblance of oil pressure just as we were getting ready to leave. Nancy was driving our 71 Chevy pickup with a 8 ft. camper on it. We looked as bad as when my parents moved to southern Oregon in 1949. There should have been a crate of chickens tied on somewhere just to complete the effect.

It was quite a trip but at least we made it all in one day. That poor truck could hardly make it over the mountains, even the little ones.

We found a mobile home in Sequim to rent and it was a pretty nice place and at the time we thought it was great because it was right next to the school. Boy did I get an education from that. You see, I had led a fairly sheltered life when it came to members of the fairer sex. That is I had no sisters or other family members except my mother to educate me on what the weaker sex was really all about. And she didn't tell me. Sugar and spice and everything nice??? NOT! But it was interesting and looking back on it a lot of it was really pretty funny but that just goes to show how much my sense of humor has improved now that I'm older.

I pulled the 428 motor out of the Thunderbird shortly after arriving. I took it out to my brother in law's farm and pulled it with the front loader on one of his tractors. I disassembled it on my back porch in town and took the block into town and had it boiled out and prepped it and had cam bearings put in etc. When I went to pick it and my rings, bearings gasket set and a new cam and lifters up I met a man who was also buying some parts. We got to talking and we introduced ourselves and it seemed that he had known my wife and her family for ever and he was a neighbor. He had a back yard shop and he convinced me to bring my car and engine over to his place and put it back together and he would help me put it in. That was the start of a 35 year friendship with him and his family. I'm sad to say he passed away a couple of years ago.

We really needed two vehicles so we could both work and one Saturday after I got the Thunderbird fixed Nancy and I went for a drive in it leaving the girls and my 71 Chevy pickup at home. When we got home a neighbor called to chat and asked me if I had got my pickup fixed. I said there was nothing wrong with it. Oh he said, I thought there might be when I saw the hood up this morning. I said no that I was just checking the oil. He then said that he had seen it cruising up and down the dead end road we both lived on all day. I thought about that for a moment said thanks I'll talk to you later, hung up and said "CHERYL. I WANT TO TALK TO YOU." Cheryl came in and said "What?" I asked her if she had been driving my pickup that day and after thinking about it for a second she said that when I had bought the pickup I had said it was the family's truck and she was part of the family and could drive it if she wanted to. Before I could say anything she ran in the bedroom and locked the door. I didn't even find out until just a short time ago that her and her boyfriend took it out another time and tried to see how much rubber they could lay with it. It had a 350 with a 4 speed duel exhaust and a four barrel carburetor. I wondered why those tires wore out so fast. Actually though, this sounds not unlike some of the things I did when I was young so what goes around comes around I guess.

Our house seemed to be a safe house for playing hooky. Since Nancy and I both worked the house was empty all day. One day I came home from work tired and wanting a cold beer. There was no beer, not even one and the empty cans were in the garbage. Of course they denied knowing anything about it. One day I came in the back door and they didn't know I was there and they, along with some friends were in the living room smoking. That, after all the fussing they had done about their mother and I smoking. At that time everybody smoked and the term "second hand smoke" hadn't been invented. They were probably our cigarettes too. I don't recall. One day Cheryl called me from school and said she was sick and would I please come get her. But, she said, will you please park a block away 'cause I don't want any of my friends to see me getting into that ugly Thunderbird. Shortly after that she wanted me to supply transportation to a dance for her and a girlfriend. I took them in the Thunderbird. Her girlfriend just couldn't believe what a cool car it was. The girlfriend went to school the next day and told all their friends what a cool car it was. I never heard any more about the "ugly" Thunderbird.

One day I got home early and I saw the girls and their friends coming across the field from the school. They came in the house and headed for Cheryl's bedroom. That was normal and I never gave it any thought. They usually went back there and listened to music. I believe I was between jobs just then and was looking at help wanted ads in the paper and never gave it any thought when I saw Cheryl and her friends go back out the patio door and head for the school again. Shortly after that Nancy got home and after the usual pleasantries, (Haven't you got a job yet?) she said she had to fix something on her nurses uniform and went to retrieve her sewing machine that she had stashed in Cheryl's bedroom. I heard her open the door, say" oh excuse me", then," WHAT THE HELL AM I DOING?" Then "YOU GET YOUR CLOTHES ON AND GET OUT OF THIS HOUSE." Shortly after that a boy that I didn't know and a girl that I didn't know both looking sheepish and somewhat rumpled ran out the door and headed for the school. Naturally Cheryl caught hell for it when she got home and just as naturally she didn't think she did anything wrong. Now that's funny, and the older I get the funnier it is. I guess you shouldn't take life to seriously. Cheryl is married now, has a grown son, works in a hospital and is also going to college.

She is well on the way to being a Registered Nurse. Janet is married and went to college to be a special ed teacher and is employed as such. Oh, by the way. Cheryl drives a new BMW sports car and she won't let me drive it.

I got a job right away working for a local developer building houses. Nancy went to work for a retirement/nursing home conglomerate called Dominion Terrace. We built a couple of houses in the Agnew area and a couple in the Heights above Port Angeles. This was in 1975 I believe. Washington just barely had building codes then. If they even had inspections then I don't remember it. I know if we didn't like the blueprint we just changed it. I worked for Larry Caldwell and another builder but things dried up in the winter so I went to work for a shop called Quality Automotive. It was about halfway between Sequim and Port Angeles. It was an easier trip in the winter anyway I thought. I didn't work there long before I started getting nervous about the dishonesty that I was a part of just by working there. Someone would come in with a car that had some problem with the engine like maybe needing a tune up or the carburetor rebuilt or a timing chain or something and the boss would convince them that they needed a new engine. Then they would send the parts puller out in back and pull a used engine out of some old wreck, steam clean it and spray bomb it and have me put it in and sell it to them as a new engine. Then they would fix what was wrong with the other engine and sell it to someone else. The guy that ran the shop was a pretty good transmission man and he would in his spare time put a kit in an old transmission and sell it as being rebuilt. We had a lot of repeat customers. (*people coming back and yelling at us.*) I finally got fed up and found another job at another shop in PA and hoped that would turn into something.

They had their own race car that I got to work on and the owner was into turbochargers and such. One of the big deals at this shop was putting turbochargers on 6 cylinder mustangs (of which there was a lot of them around.) A mustang 6 with a turbo could blow the doors off a V8. He had a ford pickup with twin turbochargers on it. Wow. I don't know why he couldn't be honest. He had lots of business. What he had hired me for was to install after market manifolds, carburetors and headers on customers cars. I did enjoy that but the boss would convince loggers that their 4X4 390 ford pickups needed a valve job when they didn't. If he couldn't get away with that he would sell them a tune up with spark plug wires that was not needed then put universal wires on that was too long and wire tie them to hoses or anything else to keep them from shorting out on the exhaust manifolds. When I tried to put them on right and make them fit the factory wire loom he said I was taking too much time. Finally he screwed up though. He bought a great huge lathe at auction that he insured for a large amount of money and told us he was going to teach us how to run it. Then a few weeks later he told somebody, I don't know who, that he was going to burn the place down for insurance money. So one Sunday morning he torched it and walked out the door and was promptly put in a squad car while the waiting fire dept. put the fire out. If he hadn't told somebody he was going to do it he might have gotten away with it, though I doubt it. So then I found a job through the local Union hall working in a small sawmill in PA. That lasted until spring.

As I said at the beginning of the Sequim experience, It doesn't rain, the wind doesn't blow it doesn't freeze hail or snow. I was building a china hutch out of some pretty plywood panels that I had found there and it was coming along really good. All I needed to finish it was some glass doors and glass shelves. It was made from ¾ hardwood plywood and was fairly heavy. The wind came up one day and blew it clean out in the middle of the back yard.

I had studded snow tires on my pickup all ready for winter. She told me it was illegal to run studded tires in Washington so I took pliers and pulled them all out. Well first it snowed than we had an ice storm and I couldn't get out of the driveway. The Thunderbird however had posi traction so I took it to work and while setting at a stoplight I could hear the cars going by in front of me, rattle, rattle, rattle. Studded tires are not legal huh? OK.

Chapter Thirteen: Home Again

◇◇◇◇

The next spring I took the pickup and drove back to Oregon. They were just starting a new swing shift and needed a crew. I went right to work and worked all the overtime I could get for a month. I needed a check for $900.00 to fly to Seattle, rent a U Haul and move my family back home. Nancy kept working but gave notice and her and the girls spent a month packing and rented a U-Haul truck. I flew into Seattle, she picked me up and took me to Sequim. The truck was mostly packed so we got right on the road. She drove the Thunderbird and I drove the truck and back to Glendale, The Robert Dollar Co. and our Hippy house we went.

It was good to be home again however the guy that had rented my house from me didn't care much for me coming back. He got mad 'cause he had to move and pulled a knife on me over at the mill one night. Nothing came of it as he thought better of it and just put it away. I did feel bad for him but I couldn't find any place else to live. I had told him when I rented it to him that this might happen though. He moved over to Grants Pass. His wife was from there and I think they liked it better anyway.

I was back to being the tail sawyer again but at least the sawyer was a friend of mine. The last guy I'd worked with didn't seem to care if the tail sawyer got hurt or not. In fact he said as much. It was very dangerous. That was an easy job to get hurt on. I did get hurt on it, twice. The first time was shortly after I learned to do the job, the sawyer dropped an 8 ft cant and came back with the carriage before it was clear and jerked it right into me and smashed the muscle in my leg. The next time was another 8 ft cant that hung up and wouldn't go down the roll case and it being late and I was tired I thought the roll case was turned off and I stood in front of it and pulled it down onto the roll case. It took me down the roll case and smashed my leg against the backstop. That leg is still numb from that accident. We stayed there for about a year that time and Nancy caught me at a weak moment and talked me into trading off my Thunderbird, which I loved for a1974 yellow and black Road Runner with a 360 and a 4 speed. That was fun. She loved that car. She would drive it to work and I could hear her going through the gears all the way to town, about three miles. (It had wicked loud pipes.)

I had gone to the trouble to learn something when I was there before and I was no longer happy just being a sawmill flunky, especially when I got hurt. I didn't need that. I started looking and found a filing job in Northern California working for Louisiana Pacific. The girls had decided they had enough running around so they went back to Sequim. They were of an age where they were going to do what they wanted. Their brother had got a place so they moved in with him. Debbie had stayed in Glendale when we moved back to Sequim so she elected to help us move to California. Another U Haul, cats and dogs and away we go.

This time I was driving the U Haul. Debbie and Nancy was taking turns driving the pickup and the Road Runner. We did pretty good until we got to Weed California. I pulled into an easily accessible gas station to get gas in the truck and they decided to go see what Weed looked like and we were supposed to meet at the next rest area.. I never saw them again for the rest of the trip. I waited at rest areas about a half hour or so at each one I came to. Finally I decided they must have passed me so I drove to Willows and then another 20 miles on out to Elk Creek. I really hoped they would be waiting for me out at the company house we had rented but no, no sign of them. I was really quite worried. A neighbor came over and helped me unload the truck and they still hadn't showed up. Finally I went to the neighbors house to use the telephone to call the State Police to see if there had been an accident. Nope nothing. Finally here they come. They saw the look on my face and they got the giggles. They finally got me to laughing too. I was scared, mad, and relieved. I don't know what my face looked like. I don't think I ever really understood what happened to them. I finally stopped trying to. I know that when Debbie and Nancy get together anything might happen.

Elk Creek California. That was an experience. That was the most backwards town, if you can call it that that I've ever called home. I used to think Glendale was bad but Elk Creek was still in the 40s. They still had party lines and if you wanted to call long distance you had to call the operator. They had a general store/post office/bar/gas station, and like when I was a child in Union Oregon, they had cattle drives right past our house. I have never seen as many or as varied species of bugs. Some could pack you off and others would come right through the window screen, and they would bite. It was hot, very hot.

Al Gore hadn't coined the term Global Warming yet. If he had I might have believed it then. It never got under a hundred. You actually got used to it. When you got up in the morning 100 felt cool. California was experiencing a drought and lake Shasta was about dry. There was a recreational reservoir right there in Elk Creek and it was dry. There was no drinking water in town. We had to haul it from Willows. Everybody had an Air conditioner except us. We hadn't been there long enough to have one yet. For recreation everybody would get together at someone's house that had an air conditioner and play poker, drink whiskey, and flirt with each other's wives. I kept a watch on mine as she was the prettiest one there. Sometimes they also hunted Rattle Snakes and Ground Squirrels. The rattle snakes were an absolute menace. They were everywhere. You were told not to go outside at night over at the mill without a flash light. A millwright killed one just outside the filing room door (but in the building) and I killed one with a pop bottle when it slithered into the lunch room. The roads around there were mostly just dirt and you could see snake tracks every morning. Sometimes we would go to Chico on the week end and rent an air conditioned motel room and just be cool. Gives a whole new meaning to being cool. The sawyer did that too with his wife, then they took pictures of each other running around in the nude and brought the pictures back and showed them to everyone at the mill. I don't know why they did that as neither one of them looked that good.

Shortly after I got there the foreman asked me if I liked to fish. I said of course and he gave me a rubber worm set up that he said I could catch Large Mouth Bass with, in the dozens of little half acre ponds that were around there. So the first chance I got I went down to a pond called Red Lake that wasn't too far from my house that I knew about. (watching out for rattle snakes of course.) I had a light spinning rig and tossed that lure out there and twitched it a time or two and bang, I had a fish. This went on for a couple of hours. What fun. I finally took a couple of the biggest ones home, about 2 lbs. Nancy didn't want to fry them that night as she already had something else planned so I put them in the deep sink on the porch and ran some water in it. The next day they were very much still alive so I took them down and put them back in the lake. I could catch a fish with about every cast and usually about 1 to 3 pounds so one day I decided to try the water across the lake. There were a patch of Lilly pads that I could see that I thought I could cast to so I did and my lure landed on top of the Lilly pads. I gave it a little twitch to pull it off as I was afraid it would get hung up and when it hit the water there was a big splash and something about jerked my rod from my hand. It was already about as far away from me as it could go so luckily it ran straight at me as my little light gear wouldn't have handled it if it would have had room to run the other way. I didn't have a net so instead I put my whole arm in its mouth and pulled it from the water. !t weighed 6 ½ lbs. Wow, that is the only reason I would like to go there again, to see if that lake is still there and to see if the fish have grown. I had to bring that one home and brag on it. Then we ate it. Yum.

One evening I came home at lunch time and when I walked into the kitchen I heard a dog growl. This surprised me as we didn't have a dog at the time. I looked and under the table was a brown and white Shepherd looking dog that I had never seen before. I knelt down and started talking to her and she finally came to me and let me pet her. She had come to the house hungry and looking abused that evening and Nancy had took her in and fed her. She had a definite attitude when it came to certain people. She didn't like any kind of uniform . She didn't like anyone looking ragged or unkempt such as a long haired hippy. She adopted us and we had a dog whether we wanted one or not. We both fell in love with her and she became part of our family. We just called her "Girl Dog."

We had made some friends and we probably could have eventually got used to the weather and even the rattle snakes but I guess it wasn't meant to be. I came home from work one day and Nancy was packing. I asked her what she was doing and she said she was leaving. She said she was taking her bed and her washing machine and I could go or I could stay but she was going back to Washington. She didn't like the heat, she didn't like the dirt, and she didn't like the bugs. She didn't like the rattle snakes. So we talked about it and actually I was less than thrilled with things too, I think we had been there about 9 weeks. So, I gave notice at the mill and we had a moving sale. I also made some phone calls and found another job at Longview Washington. I knew a guy who I had worked with in Glendale who was Head filer there who also said we could stay with them for a while till we found a place.

Chapter Fourteen:
Longview Washington, 1977

◆◆◆◆

We moved to Elk Creek in a big U Haul truck but after the moving sale we left in the pickup with some sideboards on it and the Road Runner. Debbie came and helped us move back to Washington. The dog and a couple of cats rode with me in the pickup. We spent the night in a rest area and the cats got out and being very tame friendly kitty's they went over to where some hippy's were camped. I never saw them again. I've always thought the hippy's ate them. They did look hungry. I curled up on the seat of the pickup and my dog slept in the floor right next to me. What a good dog. The next day we got to my parent's place in Glendale and we spent the night. The next day when we got ready to leave I had the passengers window down in the pickup and Girl Dog jumped in through the window. She thought we were going to leave her. Nancy had another cat with her named Zeb. He was a great big black and white cat that we had gotten from the humane Society in Roseburg about a year earlier. When we got to Longview he jumped out through the window in the Road Runner and we never saw him again. He was tired of traveling.

We rented an apartment after about 2 weeks staying with our friends and Cheryl showed up and was staying with us too. Then a short time after that we found a place that we could buy for $500 down and $500 per month. It had five bedrooms and it was really pretty nice. It seems a contractor had bought the place as it had a large parcel of property with it that he wanted to build houses on. He was intending to tear it down and build a new house there as well but decided that it was too nice to tear down so he made some repairs to the foundation and sold it to me for $30,000. When we got that they all came home. Well kind of. Janet was in and out then she got married the first time. Cheryl lied about her age and got a job in a restaurant and rode a bicycle with no brakes back and forth to work . Debbie lived with us off and on and then she got married and her oldest daughter was born while her and her husband were living with us. At some point in time someone was growing pot in an upstairs bed room in a closet with a grow light. I wonder if also at some point in time that my mother might have prayed that someday I would have children that would give me as many problems as I gave her and dad. It about made me believe in Karma.

Nancy got on at the mill working on clean up where I worked so that worked out pretty good for awhile. We made a lot of friends working at the mill. It was like one big happy family. We used to share rides with this one couple as well as kind of run around with them. He tended to do some pretty strange things sometimes that really kept us laughing. He and his wife had some small children so he had to get a babysitter when both him and his wife were working at the mill. One night right around the fourth of July he had bought a bunch of fireworks and not wanting to leave them out for his kids to get in trouble with he decided to stash them in the oven. Well you could probably guess the rest. He came home from work and forgot that he had put the fireworks in the oven and decided to cook a frozen pizza. He put the oven on pre heat and it was a gas oven. Firecrackers and roman candles and sky rockets started going off and blew the oven door off and set the kitchen carpet on fire and I seem to remember it blew the window out also. He called the fire department, and they got things under control all except they couldn't stop laughing. He was an alcoholic and that was the major reason he did so many dumb things and eventually it wound up costing him his marriage and his family.

While we were living in Longview I finally made contact with my daughter who I hadn't seen since she was 18 months old. She was then 14 years old. I got in touch with my ex sister in law who lived in Oregon and went to see her. She had 8 mm movies of my daughter at various stages of her life as she had been growing up and she showed them to me. I had tears running down my face as I watched those films and I finally convinced her to give me an address. I sent my daughter a birthday card and addressed it to her with her first and middle name and my last name not knowing that she had been adopted. Her mother was no longer married and they were living in a trailer park in Boise Idaho, and when her mother saw the envelope addressed that way she knew that it was from me. She did however give it to her and she asked her if she wanted to meet her real Dad. She said she did and her mother wrote me and told me I could come.

We communicated back and forth after that for a while

and she graduated from high school. I was invited to come to her graduation but didn't come because I thought I was too busy at work. I got in trouble for that. I got her a car that she was supposed to pay for. I took the loan out in her name with me as a co signer so that if she didn't pay the payments I did to protect my credit. I was at her wedding and at the birth of her second child. I was there right after her first child was born. I didn't even know she was pregnant till after the fact when her son was born. She had been told that if she got pregnant again it could kill her so she didn't tell me. I guess she thought I'd be mad. She was right. I would have been worse than that if something had happened to her. I've since decided that if she needs money, just to give it to her. I guess since I wasn't there for her when she was growing up that I owe it to her.

It's been 30 years ago now since I found her and she has made me a Grandpa 3 times over since then and sometimes the road has been rather rocky in our relationship but I'll always be eternally grateful for her aunt for reuniting me with my only daughter. Also for my wife who was instrumental in my putting forth the effort to find her in the first place and has over the years become a very good friend and sometimes almost a second mother to her. She has introduced Nancy to people as being her stepmother, although it's only been recently she has actually started referring to me as "dad". Her kids all call me Grandpa though. I am proud to say that Nancy's kids all call me their stepfather, and to Janet I'm "PaPa".

While we were living in Longview I got the bright idea to start a business. I had met a man in Sequim a short time before who had a portable pressure washer and I was impressed what it would do and how much demand there was for the service. Pressure washers were in themselves in their infancy at the time. Now you can buy them at Home Depot or even at Walmart but then you had to have one built. I borrowed the money from Dad as he was always interested in things like this too. It cost $3500.00 and it put out 1200 psi at 4 ½ g.p.m. Now 1200 psi doesn't sound like much until you look at the 4 ½ gallons per minute. The ones today that have a rating of 2000 psi doesn't have half the GPM capability. Also the outlet hose was 100 ft long with wires in it so that I could start and stop the engine from 100 ft away and change chemicals including wax from 100 ft away. I got a business license and a tax number and I was in business.

I was still working at the mill and doing my business part time which worked out pretty good since I was working swing shift at the mill. Nancy was working also but she was having some health issues and one day she informed me that she was going to have a Hysterectomy. I hadn't even known that she was having a problem. She had the surgery and it took her a few weeks to recoup and then she was back to work. Debbie and her husband was living with us then and a baby was about to be born. One afternoon Debbie told us that it was time and I rushed her to the hospital only to have the nurse send her back home again. Soon she said again that it was time and when we got to the Hospital she was sent home again. The next time I took her in I told them to keep her cause I had to go to work and when I came back after work I expected to see two of them. When I got off work that night the baby had been born and they were both fine.

One day while at work the owner of the company called me over to his office when I got to work. He told me that he was building a new mill and he wanted me to be the head saw filer there. He said he would get training for me so that I could run the filing dept just the way he wanted it. He told me where the mill was, about 20 miles down the river at Clatskanie and said I could go look at it. He said Nancy could work there also. He also said that I should not tell anyone about this. So I went to look at the mill and it looked like a pretty good thing. The Head filer and I although we had been friends hadn't been getting along well for awhile as he was drinking a lot and had been acting pretty erratic. Bob (the owner) told his day shift foreman what he had planned for me and I guess he hadn't told him to keep it quiet because he told the head filer and everyone else and since it was a Union mill the head filer filed a grievance. Bob called me to his office and gave me hell for talking about it and wouldn't believe me when I told him I hadn't and who did. I lost my temper and I gave him notice then and there.

I started trying to run my business full time then and I had good days and bad days and worse days. Some days I would make $500 in one day and some days nothing. But with Nancy working we were getting by. I had a few jobs that was bread and butter, that is repeat jobs every week. One company had me wash a fleet of log trucks every two weeks. I think that amounted to about $300 every two weeks. I needed about 2 more like that and everything else would have been gravy. Then Nancy hurt her back at work. I had to find another job.

I had heard they needed a filer at a Weyerhaeuser mill in Longview and I applied for a job there. It turned out that they had an under qualified person doing the work somewhat but although he had been threatening to quit he was still there and since it was a union job they couldn't fire him simply because he wasn't qualified to do the work. Meanwhile they hired me to pull green chain and there I was again. At least we had an income and Nancy was getting money from the state for the time being so once again we were getting by.

One of the guys that I worked with turned out to be the person who I had sold my Motorcycle to in Glendale. He was pulling Green Chain too and was painting cars on the side to make a little extra money. One night when I was at work I slipped and fell when I was pulling a particularly heavy board and hurt my back. They sent me to their company nurse and I had a big red spot in the middle of my spine. Now when I look back on it I think we both should have started going to church. We definitely needed to be saved. Nothing was going right.

While I was off with a hurt back one of my pressure washing contracts came due and I wasn't able to do it myself so rather than lose the contract I hired a guy to do it while I went along and supervised. Two weeks later the Dr. said I could go back to work on light duty and when I showed up for work they sent me home and told me to come back the next day and attend a meeting. I did and a union rep was there along with a company rep. It seems they had a man following me around with a camera to see if I was faking my bad back and they said I had been doing my pressure washing job while I had been off work, even though they had no pictures of me actually working, they had a picture of me standing beside my van. I told them what had actually occurred and they couldn't prove otherwise so they told me I could go back to work but I would be on probation. I told them to stuff it. They or nobody else was going to put me on probation ever. God that felt good, even if it meant being unemployed again.

Nancy and I talked about it and decided we had been there long enough and we put the house on the Market and bought a 2 year old thirty foot Komfort travel trailer. We sold the house for a profit and went up to Sequim for a break. We parked the trailer at her folks and had a good time visiting and just whatever for a few weeks.

There was an irrigation pond there that I went swimming in. My Girl Dog had never been in the water but she went with me and stood on the bank and barked at me all the time I was in the water. Finally I picked her up in my arms and carried her out on the dock and jumped in the water. Then we swam back to shore together. After she found out she could swim I couldn't keep her out of it. When she got too hot she would go down and go swimming by herself. We took her on a picnic once and she went down to the lake by herself and went swimming and we hadn't missed her. She wasn't used to such a large body of water and swam out too far and almost didn't make it back. I found her on the beach about half drowned.

We spent about a month there with Nancy's family and decided it was time to get on the road. We had a new van that we were pulling our home on wheels with and inside the van was our pressure washer. The plan was, to travel all over the country making a living with the pressure washer. I could make $50.00 washing a single wide mobile home in a park, $70.00 for a double wide, more for washing roof's sidewalks, and patios. Park owners really liked for someone such as I to come in and clean up their tenants properties. We thought it would be fun and it even could be profitable. Especially if we stuck to states like Oregon that did not have a sales tax and we therefore would not have to deal with a local tax code.

So we got up one morning hooked up the trailer and spent most of the day saying goodbye. I spent some time talking with my Father in law who I really had become quite close to. Over the time we had spent there I spent most of my time with him.

His name was Ero Jarvis and he along with my mother in law were second generation Finlanders. They were both pioneers in the Dungeness valley. They were both so interesting to talk to. He was an electrician and he had retired from Boeing. He had also been a lineman in Alaska when the only transportation was either snow shoes or dog sleds. He was also a dairy farmer and he had cleared the 20 acres himself to live on and milk a dairy herd and raise and care for his family on. She had been by his side through it all and had been the perfect help mate and mother to his children and had worked as hard as he had. I really hated to go as I had really enjoyed myself while we were there, but finally we took some pictures, loaded up our dog and away we went. We stopped at an RV park outside of Longview, unhooked the trailer and went to a friends house to visit and try and retrieve some things that we had loaned to them, when we had lived there. We then went back to the trailer and went to bed. It had been a long day. The next morning we had a message to call our friends. That's when we found out that Nancy's Dad had died of a massive heart attack the night before after we had left.

We hooked up the trailer, heading North, once again, but this time without the joy we'd always felt before when making this trip. When I pulled into the long driveway I felt a sense of dread. Nancy ran in the house to console her mother and to also be consoled herself. I backed the trailer into the spot that I had so recently vacated and hooked the power cord up to the receptacle that Ero had put in for me on the side of the old log Sauna. I hooked up the sewer to the temporary septic tank that he had helped me to put in a month earlier. The water hose was still there from where I had unhooked it the day before. Everything was still the same but it was forever changed in ways that nobody could yet imagine. I unhooked the van and parked it beside the trailer and started to walk towards the house. I saw his red sweatshirt hanging beside the door where he had left it the night before, where he always hung it. His son John walked out of the house also dressed in a red sweatshirt , He looked so much like his dad, in the way he walked and the way he was dressed that I lost it. I could be brave no longer. I went back to the trailer and I cried. For what seemed like a long time. Finally I composed myself, washed my face, and went in to see if I could be there for someone else to lean on.

After the funeral we stayed there for awhile and tried to decide what to do next. As I said, everything had changed. Ero was it seemed the glue that held the family together. Everyone just seemed lost without him. Nancy talked to her mother and we decided to do a little traveling. She grew up and had gone to school in Naselle Washington and she still had some Finnish friends that she had grown up with there so I bought a love seat hide a bed to carry in our van for a second seat and a bed, bolted it down and took Momma traveling. She had a good time and it took her (and our) mind off of what had just transpired somewhat but we had to come back eventually and get on with our lives. We had to spend way more time there then we really could afford and in doing so had depleted our cash that we had intended to pursue our new business venture with so there was nothing to do but for me to see if I could find another job and attempt to rebuild our finances. We still intended, maybe next summer of having a mobile pressure washing service and just traveling around all over the country.

I heard about or read about a job opening in a little cedar mill in Oregon City Oregon on the banks of the Willamette river. I applied for the job and was hired. Then I had to figure out where we were going to live. I checked with a few Mobil home parks in the area but they weren't too keen on having a travel trailer on their premise. Finally while having lunch in a small café, I mentioned to a waitress what my problem was and she introduced me to a man who had just came in. He was a professional painter and he and his family owned 10 acres not far from there. He said I could park it there on a temporary basis so he became my landlord for a short time and we also became good friends. About a month later an opening came up in a park just down river from the mill so we moved in there.

This man is one of the more interesting characters I have met in my life. Everybody just called him "Red". His face was lined and looked for all the world like a red headed Abe Lincoln. He also liked his friends to have a drink or two or three, with him and his wife, who Nancy also became good friends with. He was Norwegian I believe although I often thought he would have made a good Finlander. He and his wife really liked to go to dances. They especially liked to Polka and Schatish. Nancy also grew up with this type of dancing and she enjoyed it immensely, and as things have a way of working out, the man who was the head filer at the mill was also a Scandinavian. His name was Otto and he Played an accordion and had a small band. They played most weekends at a little club in Oregon City . Naturally that is the type of music they played and we went there about every other weekend and Red and his wife Joyce went there with us sometimes also.

Chapter Fifteen: Oregon City 1979

❖❖❖❖

A long about 1980 or 81 every one got to thinking the price of gas was atrocious (Though nothing like now) and there were articles in magazines about making your own fuel. Well Red decided that he would try it and set up a still to make alcohol. Well then he tasted it and thought it wasn't bad so then he got some recipes for making Peppermint Schnapps then Bourbon, then Gin, then Vodka then Rum. Wow. This was too good to run in the van so he drank it. When I came over I drank it too. It really was pretty good. Trouble being that after a couple of drinks I would be under the table and I would go outside to walk it off and wind up laying down in the back floor of my van and passing out. Nancy had to take me home more than once. He and his wife finally moved to Alaska to work on the pipe line which is probably the only reason I'm still alive today. I'm sure it's the only reason I'm still married.

I went to work on swing shift. That seemed to be the shift I'd worked all my life and thought it would be from then on. Otto, the head filer, really liked me and he saw that I was eager to learn and decided that I had enough natural ability that he might be able to make me into a head filer. I would try and come in early everyday so that I could pick up a little more on bench work. He had arthritis in his hands so that it really hurt him to try and level a saw with a hammer. He taught me to hammer round saws and I took care of them exclusively on swing shift. He used to leave band saws for me to level as that gave me experience plus it helped him out. When he finally decided to retire they were going to hire a filer off the street but I told them I wanted a shot at it. I did all the bench work for the next week and I got the job. Awhile later, probably two years, Otto got lung cancer. They caught it early and removed part of his lung and gave him radiation and he was in remission they said. A short time later he fell going down the stairs and broke his arm. A week later he was dead. His wife called me and asked me to be his pall bearer.

I was Head Filer in that mill for the next ten years. I sold my pressure washer to a friend so that his son could start a business in Port Angeles. An old man who I had befriended in the trailer park died and to help his wife out and to give us a little more room we bought their ten ft wide mobile home. It was exceptionally nice and we lived there for about 7 years. Living in a trailer park is really a life style all to itself. You have your own home and outside of maintenance on the trailer itself there isn't a lot to do. I lived in one of the best fishing areas in the country so I decided to buy a boat. I first bought a 14 ft Sea Swirl that was rather tippy and so Nancy was afraid of it so after we had it for awhile we traded it for an 18 ft Olympic. We both liked that. We caught Salmon in the annual spring run in the Willamette. After the Spring Salmon run is over there is a Shad run that comes up the Willamette. That was fun though not really much good to eat. I was told the Roe was good so I tried it and wasn't too impressed. Nancy and I fished in the Umpqua at Reedsport and Winchester Bay, I caught an 88 inch Sturgeon there and though it was too large to keep I got a nice picture. We also caught salmon there. We also caught Pink Fin Perch there in an area called Big Bend. They would bite on anything and when you would bring them aboard they would open their mouth and babies that looked just like them would gush out all over the floor of the boat. We would scoop up the babies and put them back in the water but I'm sure they probably got eaten by predators. The perch were really good to eat .

We finally started feeling a little cramped living in the trailer park and started looking around for something else. We finally found a double wide on an acre surrounded by Poplar trees. It was country living again and we would have some elbow room. Because it was a trailer the banks wouldn't loan money on it though so once again I had to go to my father and borrow it from him. It wasn't a handshake loan though, as there was a contract and a payment schedule. Also the interest was 10%. That sounds like a lot but that was the norm in the mid to late 80s. We didn't have any trouble selling our trailer in the trailer court and I made a good profit on it as I had fixed it up a lot since I had bought it. My carpentry skills that I had learned while building houses and the tools that I still had were standing me in good stead.

The people that I was buying the new place from was a retired minister and his wife. I had to move out of my trailer because the person that I had sold it to wanted to move in. That didn't seem to bother the old minister though, and although he had sold his place he hadn't bought anything to take its place. Luckily we had a 9 ½ ft camper that we parked in the side yard while he was contemplating where they would go. He finally bought a place in Canby and I helped him move. Before he did though A young girl named Janna, a relative of Nancy's who was from Finland and had been working as a nanny in New York came to stay with us and visit before returning to Finland. So that was Nancy and I, a Cocker Spaniel, and a grey tabby cat named Kitlingburger, and Janna. Needless to say we could have used more room but it worked out anyway. We were all easy to get along with.

We lived there until 93. I think we moved there in 87. I did a lot of work to the place. I built covered decks, put a new roof on all of it, decks too. I built a nice garage. Put in a new driveway and bought another half acre of ground right behind my place from a neighbor when he sold his place and moved up the hill. I also put in fences, and cleared blackberries as the place was infested with them and plowed and disked the field on the original place. Needless to say I didn't have as much time to go fishing as I did when I lived in the trailer park. When we moved though we made nearly $60,000 profit.

I hadn't intended to move at all. I was quite happy actually but lumber mills had started on a new age as far as Saw filing and Saw mills were concerned. Something called Stellite tipping. It was kind of like carbide tipping on round saws but more suited for band saws. Some people were welding it on by hand, but that was labor intensive and not too accurate and equipment manufacture's were in a panic trying to come up with new equipment and processes. One of the top companies was Armstrong Manufacturing in Portland Oregon. The mill in Oregon City had been chosen as a test site for this new equipment as had Simpson in Shelton Washington. Meanwhile Bennett Lumber in Princeton Idaho was trying it out and they were struggling. By this time I had a reputation with Armstrong of being an innovator and being competent. Mr. Bennett wanted to know who he could get to make this new Stellite run and I was recommended. He asked me to come up and look at his operation in Idaho plus another mill they were building is Clarkston Washington and I did. They made me an offer I couldn't refuse and I took it. Nancy wanted to move anyway.

Chapter Sixteen: Princeton Idaho, 1993

❖❖❖❖

When I went to Princeton Nancy stayed in Canby to sell our house and to take care of our house until it was sold. It was out in the country and we were concerned about vandals especially after her Mustang had been broken into when we were home. I had put my RV trailer on a rented lot and was working at the mill trying to do some much needed maintenance. Mr. Bennett had hired another head filer for the mill in Clarkston and I was looking forward to meeting him. I had been told when he would be there so I was waiting for him on a Saturday afternoon when he pulled his trailer into the mill yard. I introduced myself and told him that I had a place for him to park his trailer and lead him to it. We got to know each other over the weekend and Monday we went to the mill in Princeton and I gave him a two week crash course on running Stellite equipment. He had filed at a few other mills, the latest one being Wyoming Sawmills. He was a young family man , about 10 years my junior and we hit it off right away and became good friends. He had never had the opportunity to work with Stellite before though so I kept him at the Princeton mill for awhile to train him.

When I had taught him all I could we went to the plant superintendent and told him it was time to go to Clarkston. The company rented trailer spaces for us and we moved. It was so hot down there that we were having a rough time of it so I swapped my trailer for a larger one with a nice shower and air conditioning. Shortly after that Nancy came up as the house was sold and we put all of our things in storage 'till we had a place for it. Then my brother and his wife showed up with their trailer and dogs. They were on vacation and looking for work too. The plywood mill that he had worked at for years in Medford Oregon had shut down. About another two weeks and I had done about all I could do down there so I pulled my trailer back to Princeton. My brother pulled his trailer there also and parked it where my friend had his parked next to mine. My friend had rented a house in Lewiston and he and his wife were moving in along with help from their two sons.

My brother looked around the area and put in several applications but there wasn't really a lot of hope. That was saw mill country, not plywood, simply because the available logs were too small and the wrong kind. He was getting a pretty advanced case of emphysema and shouldn't have been in a mill anyway but Social Security wouldn't give him benefits and he couldn't retire without them, So after about 2 weeks he hooked his trailer up and headed back to Oregon. He found a job in a little remanufacturing mill for awhile with heavy sawdust and no respirator. It nearly killed him. After that though there was no question; he got his disability.

I really thought that since the area that I was moving to was a depressed economy that I wouldn't have a problem finding a place to live for a reasonable amount of money. That was wrong too. I couldn't find any place to live for any amount of money. Rent or buy. In the fall the mill offered to sell me a place on Hatter creek that they had bought for the timber that also had a house and a barn on it. I really liked the place but it had 10 miles of really bad road to get to it that the county did not want to do anything about so after renting it all winter I made a deal to buy the lot in town we had been living on for $1500,(If you can call anything in or around Princeton Idaho a town.) and we bought a new doublewide and had a contractor pour a foundation for it. I also had a well drilled and later had my step son come up and help me and we built a nice two story garage with a Gambrel roof. I just about had my nest made again.

We really enjoyed Idaho while we were there. We had come from two of the most Liberal states in the country: Washington and Oregon. We had also both been raised by parents that were staunchly Democrat and thought that Franklin Roosevelt was the greatest thing that ever was. We found ourselves in a Conservative state working for a Conservative employer and literally surrounded with Conservatives/Republicans. Up until then I thought (since my Dad was a Democrat) that I was a Democrat. Actually, although I always voted, I really didn't know what I was. I did think that Ronald Reagan was a great president and that Bill Clinton had shamed the country. It wasn't exactly a condition of employment but there were political rallies and dinners in Moscow that we were expected to attend. We learned a lot while there and when we moved back to Washington we had our eyes opened.

We also had a lot of fun fishing and just exploring the country. It seemed that everywhere we went we would see wildlife. One thing we saw a lot of that neither of us had ever seen before was Moose. We saw them close to where we lived.

There was a cow and a yearling that I would see sometimes while riding my ATV on the back side of the wheat field back of our house. We sometimes saw Moose when on our way to Coeur d'Alene. The first time we thought it was a horse at first glance and we turned around and went back. It was a cow moose and she looked pretty ragged since she was losing her winter hair. Once when on my way to Coeur d'Alene early in the morning on company business I saw one I would rather not have. The road was icy and I was driving my brand new pickup. It had 300 miles on it. A cow moose stepped out on the road about 20 yards ahead of me and promptly fell down spread eagled on the icy blacktop. A chip truck was coming up the hill in the other lane and I had nowhere to go. I tried to stop but the road was so slick that all I did was slide. I did get slowed down and she got up and then fell again just before I hit her. My bumper hit her hip hard enough that it pushed the bumper back about two inches and her head came back and made a small dent in the fender. Her back foot was under the front of the pickup and kicked the four wheel drive actuator off of the differential. My friend who was riding with me, the chip truck driver and myself, worked to get the moose back on her feet which we finally did. Her back was as high as the top of my head. The top of her head was probably close to 8 feet high. You would have no idea how big those things truly are until you are standing next to one. She was confused and tried to get in the open door of my pickup. We finally got her across the highway and she went over the bank and stood down below the road looking at us. I thought she would be ok so I headed for Coeur d'Alene. The Chip truck driver radioed Fish and Game and I found out later they tracked her down and shot her. I had left my name and phone number but they never tried to contact me.

Most of the people I worked with were hunters and virtually all of them owned ATVs. A friend who was about ten years older than I had a Honda 300 4 trax and his grown son who didn't live with him had one also and left it at his Dads place. Jack (the father) liked to ride but not by himself as he had some medical issues, so he asked me to come out and ride with him. After learning how to ride I finally broke down and bought one of my own. I bought a 300 cc Arctic Cat. I also bought a snow plow for mine. That came in very handy in that country. I lived right on the edge of forest service land, with Just a wheat field between us and it. I could be riding trails in 5 minutes after leaving home. I had neighbors who also had ATVs who I used to go riding with. There was one man who I worked with and one who was an electrician who worked in town. I went with the electrician riding one day and the trails were pretty dusty so I dropped back a ways so I wouldn't be eating dust so bad. As I came around a bend in the trail and started down hill, suddenly there was a bull moose standing on the trail in front of me. I stopped. Not more than 50 feet separated us. He put his head down and shook his horns at me. That was a warning. He was a fairly young one. He had a good rack of horns, not enormous but he looked pretty formidable anyway. I slowly backed my ATV around sideways in the trail, put it in low gear and just watched him, ready to take off if he charged me. Finally he turned his head down the hill, took a couple of steps that way and over the bank and he was gone. This exchange had probably taken ten minutes but it felt like an hour. I took off down the hill past him as fast as I could go before he changed his mind. Down the hill probably a couple of hundred yards I came upon my riding companion. He had his camera out and was pointing up the hill. There was another one that was probably the sibling to the one I saw. Same size and looked just like it. It was a lot farther away from him than the one I'd seen had been from me.

Something I want to emphasize is that these animals are not "Bambi" and they're not afraid of man and they are dangerous and entirely unpredictable. Bull, Cow, it makes no difference. They can and will stomp you into the ground. You especially have to watch a cow with a calf. That mother instinct will take over and you are in trouble. One of the most dangerous things you can do is hit one with your car or pickup while they are standing up. They are so big and tall that they will come right through the windshield. Many people have died in such a collision in that part of the country. They don't really have any natural enemies, or they didn't until the wolves came back and now I imagine the wolves are taking some calves and old ones, but they are really becoming numerous and the hunting is so restricted that I wonder if it wouldn't be a good Idea to relax some of the hunting restrictions. You can only have one tag in your lifetime and then only if you are lucky enough to be drawn. No out of state tags are issued. I met people while I was there that had lived there all of their lives and had applied for a tag every year after they had been old enough to hunt and had never been drawn. I went Elk hunting with some people in 1999 and In one weeks time of hunting every day I saw one bull Elk and two Bull Moose in different places, one BIG bull by himself and another one several days later with a harem of cows and yearlings. Another day we saw a yearling by himself. I would surmise from that that there were more moose than elk in that area.

The White Tail deer population is quite large too. I think it was the winter of 2000 that we had a particularly large amount of snow and quite cold temperatures. The ranchers in order to save the wildlife took round hay bales and broke them and spread them out on the foothills surrounding their farms. This was visible from the highway going through town and another place out of Princeton going up Hatter creek. There was literally hundreds of deer feeding. They were impossible to even count. It is amazing that that many animals in one area can remain virtually invisible most of the time. It makes me wonder about these people who claim to be able to count Spotted Owls.

Fishing was a lot of fun too. I especially liked to fish at a lake called Dworshak Reservoir on the Clear water river. In the summer time after they had grown up you could catch Kokanee upwards of 15 inches, and the limit was 20 fish per fisherman. Small Mouth Bass fishing was also amazing. Lake Coeur d'Alene had a lot of Kokanee also, probably too many as they never attained any size. Fish and game tried to solve that problem by planting Chinook salmon in the lake thinking they would eat up some of the numerous juveniles and instead wound up with a spawning population of Chinook salmon. They even have salmon derbies now. Then they planted Northern Pike with the same thoughts in mind and now they have a really good Pike fishery. The Pike grow to 40 plus inches and are fat as butterballs from feeding on Kokanee and Chinook Smolt. There are still a lot of Undersize Kokanee though. Then you had the Snake River at Lewiston and also the Clear water River that feed into it. Great Salmon and Steelhead fishing. The Steelhead there are as large as Salmon. They run 18 to 20 plus pounds. They also legally fish for them at night. There are several small lakes around that freeze in the winter and are good ice fishing. I had the opportunity to try that also: That was fun.

As they say, all good things must end though. Due to a falling out between myself and the sawmill manager I tendered my resignation, sold my house and moved back to Washington. I was getting close to retirement anyway and had built up a sizeable 401K nest egg while there.

Chapter Seventeen:
Hoodsport Washington, 2002

❖❖❖❖

We had made a deal to purchase a piece of property in the Lake Cushman water shed area to build a house on and at least there was a RV port on the property complete with a RV to live in. The property had been originally set up as an RV camping spot with three complete RV hookups including telephone line and satellite TV hookup. However this had been put in some years ago and wires were all corroded and not functional. There was however a 3 bedroom septic tank system, a 300 ft. deep well complete with a water treatment system, outbuildings, (gambrel roof storage buildings) concrete slabs in usable areas, a woodshed; complete with wood, and picnic tables. At least it gave us someplace to be while we made plans for our future.

I wasn't old enough to draw Social Security yet though Nancy was so after a while we decided I'd better find a job. Nancy found an ad in the local area paper saying that Simpson was looking for a filer so I applied and was hired almost immediately. That was a stroke of luck. Since we now would have an income again we started making plans for a house. First the RV port would have to go as that was where all of the plumbing and wiring was that would need to be connected to the new house. Since all of that needed to go, we bought a used 40 ft. park model trailer that was in pretty sad shape from a local dealer and I set about making it once again livable. The carpet was a disaster so it came out. I replaced it with Vinyl laminate. The bedroom carpet was usable with a good shampooing so I saved that. The bathroom vinyl was ok so that was thoroughly cleaned and saved. Appliances were gone so new range and refrigerator was purchased. The sliding glass main door wouldn't slide so I had to replace all of the rollers and have the screen door rescreened. The floor vents were full of candy, toys hair ribbons and hay, black water holding tank had a 1 liter plastic pop bottle in it. Roof air worked great (Thank God) as did the water heater and furnace. My friend came from Idaho and bought the other trailer.

The park model was nice to live in after all of that work on it We had already decided what house we were going to put here so we knew the area it would have. I knocked the supports out of the RV port (That was made from cedar logs with a metal roof) hooked my pickup on to it with a chain and pulled it down. We then dismantled it saving what I could for future use, cleaned up the area and called the contractor to start excavating and pouring concrete.

We got the framing finished and the roof on about time for the seasonal rains to begin; it had gotten a little rain previously though so it still had to dry out some before insulation and drywall could go in. I had installed a chimney so I purchased and put in a wood stove and ran it night and day for a week and dried it out. I also had put in a propane fired furnace that was ready to go by when the dry wall was being installed. By this time I was working graveyard shift at the mill so I had time in the evening before I went to work to work on the house. I put the flooring in the house, installed the cabinets, put lights in, installed all of the interior doors, toilets and sinks. Nancy painted doors, walls, ceilings, wood trim and anything else that needed painting. We moved in the next spring about a year after we had started. We advertised the park model and sold it in about a week and made money on it. I worked for a couple of years after we got the house built and one evening at work I had an appendix attack and had to have it removed . They didn't cut me open, just a couple of tiny little nicks so I was back at work in a few days. Then my shoulder started hurting and I was unable to lift a saw with it and so I was unable to work. I went to an orthopedic surgeon and after X-Rays and a M.R.I they said that I had a badly torn Rotator Cuff and I would need surgery. I was off work with that for about 2 months and when I came back I found that the Head Filer had gotten ill while I was gone and he had been let go. Everything was changed it seemed and they were going to make a person Head Filer who absolutely was not qualified for the job. He started telling me how it was going to be as soon as I got back to work and after giving it some thought I decided it was time for me to go. I went down and signed up for Social Security and was looking forward to my retirement. Then my hip started bothering me.

My hip continued to get worse. The Dr. who had operated on my shoulder subjected me to multiple X-Rays and various imaging devices and said he could find nothing wrong with my hip, however he thought they should replace it anyway. I said thanks but no thanks and went to another Dr. I got the same imaging from him and the next one and the same diagnosis and the same "I think we should replace your hip anyway." It got so bad I could hardly walk and used a cane to walk at all. I had multiple Cortisone injections and that would make me pain free for about 30 to 45 days. Finally the first Dr. called me and wanted me to come see him. He said he thought I had an "Impingement." He said he could fix it and so since the Cortisone no longer seemed to be working I decided to give it a try. He operated on me and cut the hip socket open and took the ball out and scraped and reshaped it and put it back in and wired the socket closed again. After a couple of months time I had decided that it hadn't worked. It was as bad, or even worse than it ever had been. About that time a new orthopedic surgeon had relocated to Shelton and advertized that he was in town. I called his office and made an appointment. He checked me out and took some X-Rays and told me that what was wrong was my hips and consequently my lower back was out of alignment and I needed physical therapy at least 3 days a week. I went for therapy for about 90 days and I was noticeably better. I had a list of exercises that I did at home that seemed to help but I seemed to have reached a plateau. Then one day I was at my neighbor's house and I mentioned to him that I had seen a inversion table advertized and was considering purchasing one. It turned out that he had one and asked me if I would like to try it. Of course I did and my back and my hip felt a lot better the next day after only spending about 3 minutes on it.

I tried it every few days after that when my back would bother me. One day a catalog came in the mail with one advertized for $129.00. I bought it and when it arrived I started using it for a few minutes each day. Within a few weeks I could look in a full length mirror and I could see myself standing straight, probably for the first time in my adult life. Several friends who I attend church with have stopped by and tried the inversion table out and all but one has said they feel better or even down- right great. I enjoy the feeling of being able to give something back to my fellow man; especially something that doesn't hurt.

There is a young man who goes to my bible study group who is going through some of the same issues I went through as a young man. He had been a truck driver and has since lost his license due to a DUI. He has about run out of unemployment and also will soon be homeless. I will talk to him and try and help him to make a different choice. Perhaps he needs to learn that he is responsible and only he can turn his life around. It makes me wonder if there's not a reason why I'm where I am today.

Well now I'm 68 years old. I feel better than I've felt in years. I'm getting bored and actually thinking of going out looking for another job; I've actually put in a couple of applications on line, and I believe that with all of the years experience I have that I have something valuable to pass on; but first I think I have a story to tell that needs telling. All of my transgressions actually spanned only about four years though it certainly seemed longer than that at the time, and though I will say; it has been an interesting, and in some respects, a fun ride there are surely some things I'd change If I could have a do-over; for instance, I would love to have another chance at a military career. The seizures were a problem but at the time they exposed themselves I had already burned my bridges.

There were lots of choices I made that would have changed my whole life if I had made a different one. At that point in my life I didn't know or care about such things. Now I consider myself a patriot and when I meet a soldier I always make it a point to thank him for his service. I do know; however, that although I can't undo a moment of those years I can cherish the good years when I was making good choices and always make good choices in the future. I've still managed to have a good life; have a satisfying career, marry a good woman and raise some great kids. I suppose that's more than some and I'm thankful. I recently got Jesus back into my life. He was always there especially after that AA meeting so long ago, but I wasn't being all that I could be in that respect, until recently. I go to church every Sunday now and go to bible study at least once a week, sometimes twice. I have more friends than I can count; I've never had that before and it feels good. I've learned that I was always a sinner even when I thought I was being good. It does feel good to have your sins forgiven; and if Jesus can forgive my sins, maybe I can forgive them as well.